THE VICTORIANS

English literature in its historical, cultural and social contexts

Aidan Cruttenden

Evans

EVANS BROTHERS LIMITED

Published by
Evans Brothers Limited
2A Portman Mansions
Chiltern Street
London W1U 6NR

VISIT OUR WEBSITE
www.evansbooks.co.uk

Reprinted 2006

Printed in China by WKT Co Ltd

British Library Cataloguing in Publication Data

Cruttenden, Aidan
    The Victorians. – (Backgrounds to English Literature)
    1. English literature – 19th century –Juvenile literature
    2. Great Britain – Intellectual life – 19th century –
    Juvenile literature
    I. Title
    820.9'008

    ISBN 023752256X
    13-digit ISBN (from 1 Jan 2007) 978 0 237 52256 8

Editor: Nicola Barber
Consultant: Dr Andrzej Gasiorek, Lecturer in 19th- and
               20th-century English Literature at the University
               of Birmingham
Design: Simon Borrough
Production: Jenny Mulvanny

The publishers would like to thank Christine Hatt for her help
in the preparation of this book.

Acknowledgements
Cover: The Bridgeman Art Library
p.5   The Royal Collection © 2001, Her Majesty
        Queen Elizabeth II
p.13:   The Bridgeman Art Library
p.21:   The Bridgeman Art Library
p.25:   The Bridgeman Art Library
p.37:   Reproduced by permission of the National Trust
        Photo Library
p.39:   Laing Art Gallery/Tyne &Wear Museums
p.53:   The Bridgeman Art Library
p.55:   Reproduced by permission of the Board of
        Trustees of the National Museums and Galleries
        on Merseyside (Lady Lever Art Gallery)
p.57:   Copyright © the Tate Gallery
p.61:   Copyright © the Tate Gallery
p.67:   The Bridgeman Art Library
p.79:   the art archive

£9.99

SFC06140

CONTENTS

1. THE VICTORIAN AGE

What is 'a Victorian'? Defining the 'Victorian age' is more than just identifying a span of time from the 1830s to the beginning of the 20th century. It is a question of capturing the essence of people's lives at the time – their ideas and their culture. The period was full of contrasts and contradictions, and different writers responded to their times in very different ways. In this chapter, we introduce some key features of the 'Victorian age' and provide a brief overview of the political history of the period. Further chapters in this book deal with the major issues which are likely to be found in Victorian literature, including religious matters, education, and the arts.

The period between 1815, when the Battle of Waterloo finally ended Napoleon's hopes for European domination, and 1914, when the whole European system of interrelated and interdependent monarchies and nations collapsed into the trauma of the First World War, was generally a peaceful one. There were some conflicts, notably the Crimean War (1853-6; see box page 16), and the war between France and Prussia (which became the nucleus of modern Germany) in 1870. There was some civil unrest in Britain, and the year 1848 saw revolutionary uprisings in Paris, Budapest, Milan and other large cities. Mostly, however, and particularly in Britain, this was not a time of war.

The Victorian age was, nevertheless, a time of change. Fundamental changes in society were mirrored, or caused, by developments in technology and in scientific and economic thought. In 1831 the population of England was 13.8 million, in 1901 it had more than doubled to 32.5 million. Industrial cities grew most quickly. The population of Manchester (see page 19) expanded from 75,000 in 1801 to 645,000 in 1901, Birmingham from 71,000 to 760,000 in the same period. These tenfold increases underline the effects of the so-called 'Industrial Revolution', which began in the 18th century and had changed the face of Britain by 1900. However, industry was still labour-intensive in spite of the increases in productivity made possible by technological advances. This was the main reason why so many people flocked to manufacturing towns.

THE ROYAL FAMILY

Victoria came to the throne in 1837, aged 18. The monarchy was unpopular at the time: Victoria's uncles had been particularly disliked, George IV for his debauched behaviour and William IV for his tendency to interfere in government affairs.

Victoria married Albert in 1840 and they tried, with some success, to create an image of the perfect married couple (see illustration opposite). Albert's organisation of the Great Exhibition in 1851 was much admired, but when he died ten years later, Victoria withdrew from public life. In 1864 a notice satirically stated that Buckingham Palace was 'to be let or sold, in consequence of the late occupant's declining business', and republicanism became popular and respectable. Victoria's relationship with her Scottish manservant John Brown led to her being nicknamed 'Mrs Brown'.

Later in her reign, however, the Queen (who was also the Empress of India from 1876) became more of a splendid figurehead, even though political changes meant that she had less real power. Her Golden and Diamond jubilees in 1887 and 1897 were evidence of a remarkable turnaround in royal popularity. The Queen's private, austere nature now seemed less of a problem – in fact it was seen as dignified and appropriate to the ceremonial head of so large a state.

Sir Edwin Landseer
Queen Victoria, Prince Albert and
Victoria, Princess Royal (1840-5)
While Prince Albert was alive, the Royal Family was
often portrayed as a cohesive unit, well able to
uphold the family values that were also highly valued
in the literature of the 1840s and '50s.

Two keynotes: the pace of change and nostalgia

In this time of change, two related issues preoccupied the Victorians. The first had to do with the pace of change, the second to do with nostalgia for what those changes were replacing or had swept away. What concerned many intellectuals and educated Victorians, including novelists and poets, was to ensure that change was gradual and controlled. Ambivalence is a common feature of the period; many people viewed progress with mixed feelings. They saw technological and social change as inevitable and usually desirable, but they also feared its consequences and worried greatly about what would happen if reform turned into revolution. Even so, the spirit of the age could hardly be called conservative. There was a constant push forwards towards a better future. The statistician G.R. Porter wrote in *The Progress of the Nation* (1836-43) that he had witnessed 'the greatest advances in civilisation that can be found recorded in the annals of mankind'. The key for many Victorians was to ensure that these advances were regulated so that the social order remained intact. For example, the last prime minister of the period, Lord Salisbury, was extremely enthusiastic about the power of electricity to improve society. He was nevertheless completely opposed to social revolution.

Change inspired both enthusiasm and regret for what had been lost. In particular, there was regret that the modern, industrial world was more uncertain and less easily knowable than an older social order in which values, beliefs and position in society were seemingly fixed and unchanging. In the 19th century, belief in God was being challenged by scientific advances. Social reform, technological change and quicker travel all produced a more mobile society.

It is therefore not surprising that in all art forms there was a renewal of interest in the medieval period, when faith in an unchanging God was apparently simpler and society apparently less problematic. This interest gave rise to Alfred Tennyson's evocation of Arthurian legend in *Idylls of the King* (see box page 56), to the Pre-Raphaelite paintings of Sir John Everett Millais, Dante Gabriel Rossetti and William Holman Hunt (see page 54), and to the Gothic architecture of Augustus Pugin (see page 60). It is also not surprising that communities at the point of change often feature in Victorian novels. Hayslope in George Eliot's *Adam Bede*, the town of Middlemarch in Eliot's novel of the same name, Eltham in Mrs Gaskell's *Cousin Phillis*, and Mellstock in Thomas Hardy's *Under the Greenwood Tree* are all old-fashioned communities undergoing change. Often there is a symbol of this change. In *Under the Greenwood Tree* it is the replacement of the village church band with an organ. In *Cousin Phillis*, as in many novels and indeed poems, it is the railway.

The railway is one of the most potent symbols of Victorian progress and industrialisation. In 1830 there were 600 kilometres (375 miles) of track. One of the earliest locomotive passenger services was between Liverpool and Manchester, two cities that typified both Victorian trade and Victorian industry and commerce. On the opening day of the railway, the engine, *Rocket*, designed by Robert Stephenson, did two things: it ran over and killed George Huskisson, a former Cabinet minister, and it reached a speed of 58 km/h. The second fact was seen – even at the time – as the more significant achievement. Distance and time soon came to be perceived in a new way, and the line between Liverpool and Manchester became a great artery for goods and passengers. Its opening encapsulates the mixture of amazement and fear with which railways were often viewed – awe at the possibilities for trade and travel that the 'iron road' and its 'iron horse' offered, and horror at the rather grisly end of Huskisson (whose leg was horribly mangled).

Politics – an overview

The 'Victorian age' can be broadly split into three. The first period, one of gradual reform and change, covered the 1830s and '40s and began roughly with the First Reform Bill in 1832, ending with the Chartists' last petition in 1848. The second period in the 1850s and 1860s was relatively quiet in spite of the Crimean War at the beginning (1853-6); it was ended by the Second Reform Bill in 1867. The last period began with further social reform during the '70s. The '80s and '90s were most notable for Britain's involvement outside the island of Great Britain itself, particularly for its continuing problems in Ireland and its participation in the 'Scramble for Africa', in which the whole of Africa was rapidly colonised by the major European powers.

Why does this book take its starting point before Victoria came to the throne in 1837? The movements of history do not always coincide exactly with the comings and goings of monarchs, and

— ISAMBARD KINGDOM BRUNEL —

Isambard Kingdom Brunel (1806-59) was one of the most remarkable of the great Victorian engineers. He was the chief engineer to the Great Western Railway and was responsible for the building of more than 1600 kilometres of railway line in Britain and Ireland (not to mention others in Italy). His iron steamships, the Great Britain *and the* Great Eastern, *were the largest in the world when they were launched (in 1843 and 1858). Many of his works – the suspension bridge over the River Avon at Bristol and the brick railway bridge over the River Thames at Maidenhead, for example – challenge the boundaries between 'art' and 'engineering' by being structures of great beauty.*

The main feature of Brunel's career was his readiness to push technology to the limit, and his utter enthusiasm for new ideas. If some Victorians viewed change with horror, and many with mixed feelings, Brunel was one for whom it held endless possibilities. He was keen to point out that the Great Eastern *was as much a 'machine' as a ship, and that the commander of such a vessel had to approach his job in a totally new way:*

'The man who takes charge of such a machine… must have a mind capable of setting aside, without forgetting, all his previous experience and habits, and must be prepared to commence as an observer of new facts, and seize rapidly the results.'

writers tend to reflect historical and social movements. Victorian writers were often more interested in the state of society than in anything else, and thus much of this discussion deals with social and not with political or military history. However, some events were reflected in novels and poems. Novelists, in particular, tended to set their fiction in the relatively recent past, especially if it was relevant to issues of the present day. An obvious example is George Eliot's novel *Felix Holt, the Radical* (1866) which is set at the time of the First Reform Bill (1832) and yet is of clear relevance to the Second Reform Bill, which became law in 1867 (see page 26).

Catholic emancipation, 'Captain Swing' and the Reform Act of 1832

The prelude to change was Catholic emancipation. After over 150 years of repression (see pages 65-6), emancipation gave Roman Catholics the right to sit in Parliament and hold other government posts. This was particularly significant in Ireland, at that time fully part of the United Kingdom, where the majority of the population was Catholic. The emancipation issue came to a head over the position of Daniel O'Connell, a lawyer who was elected to Parliament in 1828 as the Member of Parliament (MP) for County Clare but who, as a Catholic, could not take up his seat. Wellington's government (see box) had its hand forced, and in 1829 the reform was voted through.

By the end of the 1820s, many people agreed that the way Parliament was elected needed to be reformed, and the death of George IV in 1830 heightened the mood for reform. Many parts of the electoral system had not changed for hundreds of years. Only men were permitted to vote – women were not enfranchised for nearly a hundred years more. Rules about who was allowed to vote were different in different towns, and the system was open to corruption at all levels. It has already been noted that Manchester and Birmingham grew enormously during the 19th century, and yet neither city had a single MP before 1832. Small towns which had once been

— THE AUDIENCE AND THE TEXT —

In 1829, the young Charlotte Brontë described the scene at Haworth Parsonage as her family read the newspaper describing the Parliamentary vote on Catholic emancipation:

'O those [days from] 3 months from the time of the King's speech to the end! Nobody could think speak or write on anything but the Catholic question . . . when the paper came which was to decide the question, the anxiety was almost dreadful with which we listened to the whole affair, the opening of the doors, the hush, the Royal Dukes in their robes & the Great Duke [of Wellington, the Tory Prime Minister] in green sash & waistcoat, the rising of all the peeresses when he rose, the reading of his speech, Papa [a great admirer of Wellington] saying that his words were like precious gold, & lastly the majority one to 4 in favour of the bill.'

It is interesting to realise that the Brontës clearly listened to the newspaper (which was presumably read aloud) almost in the same way that we would listen to or watch a live debate in Parliament on radio, TV or increasingly the internet. It is clear that people in the 19th century had to be good listeners, and had to use their imagination to picture the events and scenes described in their texts.

important still had two Members of Parliament; these MPs were often closely tied to the local landowner, who thus could effectively control their votes. A well-known example of one of these so-called 'rotten boroughs' was Old Sarum, an ancient hill-fort outside Salisbury, which had been deserted for centuries. The settlement nevertheless returned two MPs to parliament, while the 'new' city of Salisbury at the bottom of the hill had no representation at all.

Events became very tense in 1830-2. Rural labourers in Kent, Sussex and other southern counties joined in a series of rather disorganised protests and riots in the name of 'Captain Swing' in late 1830. During 1831 violent disturbances brought the country to the brink of revolution. In 1832, the Reform Bill became law when the Reform Act was passed by a mere nine votes in the House of Lords. It disenfranchised many smaller towns and enfranchised some of the larger ones, and made the rules determining who had the vote the same for all parts of the country.

It is important to recognise that this Act did *not* give the vote to everybody. Women were excluded, and, as it was still necessary to have a certain amount of property in order to vote, so were many men in the new urban working class and much of the lower middle class. The Act mainly benefited the new middle class of industrialists; most people remained as far from having a real say in who governed the country as before. Aristocratic landlords still regularly checked up on the way in which their tenants voted – there was no such thing as a secret ballot.

The lack of a secret ballot meant that elections could be disorderly affairs. In December of 1832 the young Mary Ann Evans, later the novelist George Eliot, witnessed a riot in her home town of Nuneaton which she later fictionalised as the riot at Treby Magna in *Felix Holt.* Charles Dickens, as ever using humour to make a serious point, described a chaotic election at the fictional town of Eatanswill in *The Pickwick Papers* (1836-7). As with many reforms, the First Reform Act left many problems unsolved, and many questions unanswered.

The Poor Law Amendment Act and other changes of the 1830s

Further changes came with Edwin Chadwick's Poor Law Amendment Act (1834). Under the terms of this Act, 'workhouses' were set up to provide accommodation for the very poor and destitute. However, conditions in these workhouses were deliberately made as harsh and unattractive as possible, so that people would not become reliant on them and would go to find work for themselves. Many writers, including Thomas Carlyle and Charles Dickens, were strongly opposed to the Act, seeing it as inhumane and cruel. Dickens's *Oliver Twist* (1838) is a specific attack on the Act and on the

Benthamite beliefs that inspired it (see page 24), and the scene in which Oliver asks for 'more' gruel shows how the workhouses failed to address even the most basic human needs adequately.

Other changes were more welcome: slavery in the British Empire was abolished in 1833, and in the same year factory inspectors were first appointed to oversee the conditions in which people worked. Victorian factories were still extremely dangerous, but the inspectors' reports were increasingly studied and by the middle of the century many were taking health and safety issues more seriously. Literature also reflected these concerns: Bessy Higgins, in Mrs Gaskell's *North and South* (1855), describes how she developed the respiratory disease which is killing her:

> 'I began to work in a carding-room... and the fluff got
> into my lungs and poisoned me. Fluff... little bits, as
> fly off fro' the cotton, when they're carding it, and fill
> the air till it all looks fine white dust... There's many a
> one as works in a carding-room, that falls into a
> waste, coughing and spitting blood.'

Radicals were increasingly upset about the fact that the Reform Act had not gone far enough. Workers began to form themselves into trades unions (see page 41), and in 1834 a group of labourers from Tolpuddle in Dorset (only a few miles from where Thomas Hardy was born six years later) were transported to Australia for forming a union. From 1836 bad harvests led to economic depression and unrest. Victoria's accession to the throne in 1837 was immediately followed by the rise of the two main protest movements of this period, Chartism and the Anti-Corn Law League.

Chartism

The more radical of the two movements, popular among the working class, was Chartism. Its ideas dated back to the 18th century, but they had a great impact in the years just after Victoria came to the throne. It derived its name from the People's Charter of 1838, a list of six demands for reform: a secret ballot; equal electoral districts (so that very densely populated areas were properly represented); the abolition of property qualifications for MPs (so that Parliament was no longer open only to the rich); payment for MPs (so that they did not need private incomes to support themselves while they sat in Parliament); annual Parliaments; and the vote for all adult males. (The Chartists, incidentally, rejected the idea that women should be allowed to vote, although it was proposed at one time.)

The years 1838-42 were the heyday of Chartism. In 1839 a petition was presented to Parliament. Unsurprisingly, it was rejected as too revolutionary. Unrest in November of that year led to several Chartist leaders being imprisoned or transported to Australia. In 1842 a new petition carried three million signatures; again it was rejected (see pages 22 and 23).

Chartism was most popular when bad harvests led to economic depression. Better times after 1842 led to a decline in the movement; then another slump in 1848 resulted in another petition, which was ignored. This was the end of Chartism as a mass movement, though some of the leaders remained in public life. Writers had mixed feelings about Chartism. Most mainstream novelists and poets regarded it with some sympathy, but found its more militant aspects disturbing. When, in Mrs Gaskell's *Mary Barton* (1848), John Barton returns from being a delegate at the Chartist convention of 1839 in London, he finds that his wife and baby have died of starvation and fever. Gaskell's portrait of Barton is sympathetic, but there is more than a hint that he should have been looking after his family instead of indulging in dangerously radical politics (see page 22 and 23).

The Anti-Corn Law League and the 1840s

The Anti-Corn Law League represented the interests of the commercial middle class. The Corn Law of 1815 taxed imported grain. This pleased landowners, but for the urban poor it caused a problem by keeping the price of bread high. The factory owners of the League were concerned that hunger and high prices would make their workers uncooperative and encourage revolutionary ideas. In spite of its middle-class base, the League also attracted radical support, because workers would also benefit from lower bread prices. From 1840, its leaders successfully used the new penny post to organise support for their cause. Their leader, Richard Cobden, became a celebrity, although it was 1846 before Robert Peel, the Tory Prime Minister, managed to repeal the Corn Laws and abolish the duty on imported corn, at the expense of splitting his own party into 'Peelite' and 'Conservative' factions (see Glossary of Terms). None of this helped in Ireland, where potatoes, a dietary staple, were badly affected by 'blight', a rotting disease. In the years 1845 to 1849 a

——— THE PENNY POST ———

Buying a stamp and posting a letter is so ordinary an act for us that it is hard to see it as a revolutionary idea. And yet the Victorians thought, with some justification, that the introduction of the penny post in 1840 was one of the most significant achievements of their age.

The arrangement before 1840 was that the person receiving the letter paid for the postage. Regular communication was thus for the rich only, and the costs were hardly good for business. The teacher and reformer Rowland Hill argued so strongly for a cheap, pre-paid method of paying for mail that the Government put him in charge of the reform. He favoured labels to stick on to the letter – stamps – and a whole new channel of communication was opened. By the mid-Victorian period there were deliveries every hour in London, and communication was a relatively quick business compared to the days before 1840.

million people emigrated to escape the Irish famine and half a million Irish people died. As a result, Ireland was the only part of the British Isles to show a decline in population during the 19th century.

The end of the 1840s saw some further reforms. In 1846 the first grants for teacher training were made, and in 1848 Edwin Chadwick's Public Health Act was passed (this time supported by Dickens and other writers: see box page 34), although the Health Board it set up was disbanded after its first five-year term. In 1847 the Factory Act limited the working hours for children in factories to ten a day. The pace of change was slow, however, compared to other parts of Europe, where real uprisings were taking place in the 'Revolutionary Year' of 1848.

The Great Exhibition and after – 1850-70

The Great Exhibition of 1851 was an expression of confidence in the importance of Victorian Britain as a world power. The idea to hold an exhibition of manufactured goods from around the world was suggested by similar, but much smaller events already held in France, and came from the Queen's German husband, Prince Albert. The building which housed the Exhibition, the so-called 'Crystal Palace' designed by Joseph Paxton, was itself almost the most ground-breaking feature of the whole event. Designed to be constructed in pre-fabricated sections for later assembly, it anticipated many building methods later used throughout the 20th century.

The Exhibition was a great success. The novelist William Thackeray wrote in *Punch* that 'the scene I witnessed was the grandest and most cheerful, the brightest and most splendid show that eyes had ever looked on since the creation of the world.' More than six million people visited, many travelling by railway, and Queen Victoria was ecstatic, as much for the success of her husband as for the prestige gained by the country. Writing to her uncle, King Leopold I of the Belgians, she declared that it was:

> '...the *greatest* day in our history... the *happiest, proudest* day in my life, and I can think of nothing else. Albert's dearest name is immortalised with this *great* conception, *his* own, and my *own* dear country *showed* she was *worthy* of it.'

The £186,000 profit from the Exhibition was put towards establishing an area of museums and colleges in South Kensington, which did in a way 'immortalise' Albert, making his name 'dear to Science, dear to Art', as Tennyson put it in the Dedication to *Idylls of the King*. Albert himself, however, did not live to see it. He

George Gilbert Scott,
The Albert Memorial (1863-72),
London

This huge monument celebrating the life of
Prince Albert is a typically Victorian combination
of traditional religious forms with statues
celebrating contemporary art, science and
engineering.

became probably the most celebrated victim of the many diseases of Victorian Britain when he succumbed to typhoid fever in 1861. Wealth and status were no match for the old, filthy drains in Windsor Castle.

The rest of the 1850s and '60s were a quiet time politically, though not in literature and art. Change was even more gradual than before, if anything. Writers benefited from the repeal of stamp duty on newspapers in 1855 and the repeal of customs and excise duty on paper in 1861, both of which reduced the cost of books and other printed matter. Also of interest was the Act granting Jews full civil equality in 1860; several Victorian writers tried their hand at portraying Jewish characters, culminating in George Eliot's *Daniel Deronda*, in which a young man rediscovers his Jewish roots (1876). At the end of the '60s, however, there were again moves towards more fundamental Parliamentary reform. These led to the Second Reform Bill of 1867 which nearly doubled the electorate (although this was still far from representing universal voting rights, as the Chartists had wanted).

The most comprehensive programme of reform in Victoria's reign was put through Parliament in the 1870s. Perhaps the most significant measure in terms of writers and literature was William Forster's Education Bill, which was passed in 1870 (see page 48). More reforms followed. The Trade Union Act of 1871 legalised the unions, and in 1872 the secret ballot was finally achieved (it had been one of the Chartist demands of the 1830s and 40s). Benjamin Disraeli's government of 1874-80 was particularly active in social reform, including health and housing, although some cities had been taking matters into their own hands. Joseph Chamberlain (1836-1914), the Liberal (and radical) Mayor of Birmingham from 1873 to 1876, had already been at work at a local level. He proudly claimed that the city had been 'parked, paved... Gas-and-Watered, and *improved* – all as the result of three years' active work...' (see page 26).

Ireland and the Empire – 1880-1901

Ireland had been a troubled place for many centuries by 1880. The Irish had never accepted English rule, and the relationship between the two islands was at best uneasy. At worst, it was violent, and rebellion in 1798 had led to Ireland being brought under the direct control of the Westminster Parliament in 1800 (until that date Ireland had its own Parliament in Dublin). Daniel O'Connell, whose election success precipitated Catholic emancipation in 1829, tried and failed in the following years to have the Act of Union of 1800 repealed.

There were social problems too. The population of Ireland was mainly Roman Catholic, and since England's old enemies, France and Spain, were also Catholic countries, the English had become suspicious of the loyalty of the Irish over the years. Irish Protestants, except in parts of the north, tended to be wealthy landowners. Their families had been given land hundreds of years before, when England first ruled Ireland, and they now formed a class usually called the 'Protestant Ascendancy'. Many did not even live in Ireland at all. These were the so-called 'absentees' who left the running of their estates to an agent. Maria Edgeworth's novels *Castle Rackrent* (1800) and *The Absentee* (1812), which were admired by Jane Austen and Walter Scott, describe this society. Edgeworth herself was the daughter of an enlightened Protestant landlord, and cared greatly for Ireland and its people; others, like the 'absentees', were much less responsible, and the conditions in which many ordinary Irish people lived were atrocious.

Many estates owned by absentee landlords were divided into tiny plots of land on which tenant farmers struggled to raise a potato crop big enough to feed their families. The reliance on the potato as a staple food, and the fact that there were too many people for the economy to support, contributed to the disaster of the famine in the 1840s and to the massive emigration that continued throughout the century. Most large English industrial cities had an Irish district, and many Irish people were forced by hardship to emigrate to try a new life in North America, where cities such as Boston developed a strong Irish community. Even after the famine ended, the population of Ireland continued to decline – from 6.6 million in 1851 to 4.7 million in 1891.

An early novel of Anthony Trollope, who worked in Ireland as a Post Office official, describes Irish country society in the middle of the 19th century. In *The Kellys and the O'Kellys, Or Landlords and Tenants* (1848), the Ascendancy landowners, the O'Kellys, have a large house and a passion for traditional country pursuits. Their lives are paralleled by those of their tenants, the Catholic Kellys. Trollope manages to bring the novel to a satisfactory conclusion, but in reality the situation was not so simple, and real-life tenants were not so easily appeased. 'Home Rule', the various movements whose aim was to institute some form of self-government in Ireland, gained in strength in the last decades of the 19th century. Home Rule drew support from many Irish people, including Protestants such as Charles Stewart Parnell, leader, from 1878, of the Irish Home Rule Party in the Westminster Parliament.

While Parnell wanted to achieve Home Rule peacefully, other groups were more violent. Frustration was growing as, unable to pay their rents, increasing numbers of tenants were being evicted by their landlords (which the landlords had the power to do, and without compensation). In 1882 the Irish Chief Secretary was murdered by Irish nationalists in Phoenix Park in Dublin. The leader of the Liberal Party, William Gladstone, came to think that Home Rule was the only way out of this problem, and won the election of 1885 with support from the Irish Home Rule Party. The Home Rule Bill introduced in 1886 failed, however, and the 'Unionist' Liberals (supporters of the Act of Union) who split from the main party made sure that the rest of the century was dominated by an alliance of Conservatives and Unionists, who were strongly opposed to Home Rule. The Irish question remained on the political agenda throughout the 20th century, to a greater or lesser degree.

The 'Irish question' had been at issue for hundreds of years. What became the British Empire had been developing slowly since the 16th century. The first colonies in North America had been lost at the end of the 18th century, and one of the features of the later part of the 19th century was the increasing economic power of the United States. Canada, however, remained within the British Empire, with the status of a semi-independent 'Dominion'. The heart of the Empire was India, which had been under direct British control since 1858. Previously, power had been in the hands of the privately-owned East India Company, but the 'Indian Mutiny', a large-scale revolt against the British in 1857, precipitated the end of the Company's control. In 1876 the Queen was declared Empress of India. The Indian territories, the 'jewel in the crown', were commercially very valuable markets. Between 40 and 45 per cent of British cotton exports in the last quarter of the century went to India.

There were also major colonial possessions in southern and western Africa, Southeast Africa, Australia and New Zealand. In addition, Britain controlled a significant number of islands in the Pacific and Atlantic oceans, as well as Mediterranean islands such as Gibraltar, Malta and, from 1878, Cyprus. All of these are reflected in Victorian literature, even if not always in the most frequently studied texts. Matthew Arnold's younger brother William wrote an Indian novel, *Oakfield, Or Fellowship in the East*, in 1853, and Samuel Butler's satire *Erewhon* (1872) begins in New Zealand, where Butler farmed

———— 'DO AND DIE' ————

The Crimean War of 1853-6 was fought between Russia and an alliance of Britain, France and Turkey, which feared Russian dominance in the Black Sea area. It also gave rise to one of the best-known of English war poems: Alfred Tennyson's Charge of the Light Brigade. *The poem's ethos of 'Their's not to reason why,/Their's but to do and die' seems foreign to a modern world which has come to regard unquestioning duty with suspicion. It would be wrong, however, to claim that attitudes to war only became 'modern' after the First World War, or that the horrors of war were somehow discovered 60 years later by Wilfred Owen and others in the mud of the Western Front.*

In fact the Crimean War was the first in which the war correspondent played an important role. William Howard Russell, who worked for the Times, *wrote such graphically horrific descriptions of the hospital at Scutari near Constantinople (Istanbul) that his reports led directly to the appointment of Florence Nightingale to oversee the nursing of wounded soldiers. On both sides, more soldiers died of disease than in battle. The total losses were about half a million. It was ironic that the Treaty of Paris, which ended the war and established a new, but rather unstable, balance of power, was more the result of diplomacy than of fighting.*

sheep for five years. More often, the Empire provides a backdrop rather than a setting; Margaret Oliphant's *Miss Marjoribanks* (1866) is typical in that India does not appear in the novel, which is set in an English provincial town, but does provide a place for Tom Marjoribanks to work extraordinarily hard to prove himself worthy of his cousin's love.

The sun had 'never set' on the overseas dominions of the British monarch for nearly a hundred years in 1880. However, while some of the older colonies with 'white' settlements were gaining semi-independent status at the end of Victoria's reign (for example, Canada (1867) and Australia (1900)), the period from 1880 saw a new impetus from all the major European powers, including Britain, to develop their empires in Africa. This 'Scramble for Africa' is most obviously reflected in Joseph Conrad's *Heart of Darkness* (1902), which is based on events of the 1890s in the 'Congo Free State', the personal property of the King of the Belgians, Leopold II. The narrator, Marlow, is horrified by the way in which civilisation has turned into savagery in this 'heart of an immense darkness'. Appalling abuses of even the most basic human rights were beginning to be uncovered by the time the book was written.

The main motive for imperial expansion was economic. No one was in any doubt that the new colonies had the potential to make their European masters a great deal of money. The natural resources of the Congo and other parts of the colonised world were enormous: gold, diamonds, copper, sugar, tea and rubber were seemingly there for the taking. If a man's place in Victorian society was as the maker of money – and although this is a crude over-simplification, many did see his role in this way – the Empire was a place where a young man could go to find fame and fortune. It was certainly often seen as a man's world in fiction written in the 'home' country: we have seen the example of Margaret Oliphant's Tom Marjoribanks; Edwin

THE FOOTBALL ASSOCIATION

Sport in Victorian times changed quite as much as anything else in that era of change. Many major sports acquired their sets of rules during the 19th century, and football illustrates this better than any other. Football (soccer), rugby union, rugby league, Australian Rules, Gaelic football and American football are all products of the 19th century. Before the rules of these sports were codified, 'football' had a huge number of different local variations. In some the ball was handled more than in others, in some it was thrown more than in others, in all the concept of a foul was almost unknown. Kicking other players, known as 'hacking' was common (your opponent did not even have to have the ball at the time). The 'Cambridge rules' (1846), which minimised handling, and removed hacking, formed the basis of the rules adopted by the Football Association in 1863.

Team sports were especially associated with the 'public' schools (see page 45), and thus acquired a middle-class character which some, like cricket and rugby union, have not lost in England to this day. Almost all of them travelled abroad with British commercial or imperial interests. Football, however, travelled everywhere, failing only in North America where other developments squeezed out games codified in Europe. The British influence is easy to spot: Athletic Bilbao's shirts are based on those of Sunderland, Dynamo Moscow's on Blackburn Rovers, and AC Milan still uses the English version of the city's name. Most importantly, football became a working-class sport both at home and abroad. This development was clear by the 1880s, starting in the north and Scotland; by 1885 some players were allowed to be professionals. The 1899 cup final saw Sheffield United beat Derby County in front of a crowd of nearly 74,000 people.

Drood, in Dickens's last novel of the same title (1870), shows us a confident young man who is 'going to wake up Egypt a little... doing, working, engineering'. In Thomas Hardy's *Tess of the d'Urbervilles* Angel Clare, escaping from his marriage to Tess, is 'attracted' by the 'new idea' of farming in Brazil, which was not part of the British Empire but shows the same desire to make a new start on fresh soil. Some of the women who lived in the colonies also wrote about their lives: Lady Barker's *Station Life in New Zealand* (1870) and Olive Schreiner's *Story of an African Farm* (1883) are two examples.

If the Empire was seen as a source of wealth and a place of adventure, it could also be seen as a place of exotic mystery, or (more threateningly) of darkness and danger. India is the source of the 'Speckled Band', the deadly snake in Sir Arthur Conan Doyle's story, which invades the 'safe' Surrey countryside and can only be dispatched by the superior brain and logic of Sherlock Holmes (who is himself subject to an equally insidious Eastern influence – opium). Both adventure and danger can be seen in the story of a diamond stolen from the head of a Hindu idol in Wilkie Collins's *The Moonstone* (1868) and Rider Haggard's exotic romances *King Solomon's Mines* (1885) and *She* (1887). There was certainly a market for this type of writing, shown by the success of Rudyard Kipling's works with Indian settings such as *The Jungle Books* (1894-5).

By the end of the century, maps which showed foreign possessions had more red (for Britain) than any other colour; the next was blue for France. Historians cannot agree as to the main reason for the massive imperial expansion of the 1880s and '90s. Economics was a main factor, but some also point to the fact that the conquerors claimed to bring their new subjects the cultural benefits of Western civilisation and the spiritual benefits of Christianity. A common view at the time was that non-Western races actually *needed* Western control to give them order and discipline, and that the expansion of empire was thus as much a moral obligation as a desirable economic project. It reminds us of the fact that some Victorian attitudes can seem extremely different from our own.

2. THE URBAN SCENE

During the opening decades of Queen Victoria's reign, many thousands of people left the rural towns and villages where they had been born to seek employment in the factories and workshops of Britain's fast-growing cities (see page 4). Urban expansion was particularly great in certain parts of Britain: in this chapter we look at three major areas, the north of England, the Midlands and London, and their treatment in the literature of the time.

Urban areas: the north

In northern England, the Yorkshire cities of Leeds (famous for its clothing industry) and Sheffield (a steel-making centre) grew rapidly, each having a population of more than 200,000 by 1871. Bradford, further to the west in the same county, became the world's most important producer of woollen textiles. In and around Durham and Newcastle, coal-mining provided thousands of men with employment. However, it was the county of Lancashire, where the textile industry flourished, that dominated the region. At its heart was the city known as Cottonopolis – Manchester.

From the late 18th century, Manchester's businessmen built mills and factories, equipping them with steam-powered spinning machines and looms. From 1817, when gas lighting was introduced, the mills stayed open day and night. In his novel *Coningsby* (1844), Benjamin Disraeli (see box page 23) declared that Manchester was 'the most wonderful city of modern times', having 'illumined factories with more windows than Italian palaces'. These places of employment sucked in workers from the surrounding countryside, so that Manchester's

'THE RINGING GROOVES OF CHANGE'

The advent of the railway brought dramatic changes to urban and rural Britain alike, and provided an inspiration for many writers. The poet Alfred Tennyson travelled on the first passenger train to run between Liverpool and Manchester in 1830. In his poem 'Locksley Hall' (1837-8) he portrayed the railway as a symbol of Western energy, which should be welcomed, not shunned:

'Not in vain the distance beacons. Forward, forward let us range,
Let the great world spin for ever down the ringing grooves of change.'

Sadly, as Tennyson himself admitted, the words of the second line quoted were based on a false impression. While travelling, he had been unable to see the track properly, and so mistakenly believed that the train ran in grooves, like a tram. Nevertheless, the powerful image of the 'ringing grooves of change' remains a symbol of energy and progress.

Charles Dickens witnessed the 'railway mania' that assailed London in the early Victorian period, when many companies competed to build new lines into the capital. Grand new termini, such as Euston (1838) and King's Cross (1852), were also built. In Dombey and Son (1848) the novelist uses the railway to reflect two conflicting attitudes to progress. In Chapter 6, it is described, albeit with a strong hint of irony, as the 'Railroad... upon its mighty course of civilisation and improvement'. But in Chapter 55, it is seen at its most destructive when one character, James Carker, is run down by a train:

'He was beaten down, caught up, and whirled away upon a jagged mill, that spun him round and round, and struck him limb from limb, and licked his stream of life up with its fiery heat, and cast his mutilated fragments in the air.'

population grew rapidly. The development of railway transport also contributed to Manchester's expansion. Linked first to Liverpool, in 1830, within ten years the city was connected by rail to Leeds, Sheffield, Birmingham and London.

The conditions in Manchester's cotton mills were typical of those endured by industrial workers in other cities of northern England, as well as further afield. One French writer declared, in 1844, that 'overwork is a disease which Lancashire has inflicted on England and which England in turn has inflicted upon Europe'. Employees, many of them children, started work before the sun rose, and were expected to remain active for between 12 and 16 hours. Most workplaces were airless, and cotton mills, kept damp to stop the cotton threads from breaking, were breeding grounds for respiratory diseases. Machines did not have safety guards, so it was common for workers' hair or limbs to become trapped, leading to dreadful injuries.

Outside their places of employment, many mill- and factory-workers fared little better. Cities and towns were growing so fast that the demand for housing outstripped the supply. Large families had to cram themselves into badly built houses and new arrivals often had to settle for temporary shelter in lodging houses. In Leeds, it was quite normal for residents in these establishments to sleep five to a bed.

The relentless influx of people from the countryside had other damaging effects on living conditions. Existing sewage networks could not cope, with the result that human waste piled up in the streets, creating a terrible smell, as well as a danger to health. The drinking water provided, from outside taps, was often polluted, and led to the rapid spread of diseases such as dysentery, typhus and cholera. Many houses were also damp, contributing further to the bronchitis and other respiratory diseases common among mill-workers.

There were exceptions: for example, to the northwest of Bradford, a mill-owner named Titus Salt built a model industrial town called Saltaire. Opened in 1872, it provided not only housing but also schools, churches and medical care for Salt's employees.

Mrs Gaskell

One of the Victorian novelists who most accurately described urban life in England's northern counties was Elizabeth Stevenson (1810-65), who is usually known by her married name of Mrs Gaskell. Born in London, in 1832 she married William Gaskell, the minister of Cross Street Unitarian chapel in Manchester. Unitarianism was a radical belief that set its members apart from the established Church of England (see Glossary of Terms). Nevertheless, it attracted many well-educated, middle-class members. Mrs Gaskell's novels come firmly from this background.

Ford Madox Brown,
Work **(1863)**

This picture, started in 1852, shows roadworks in
Hampstead, North London. It is packed with symbolism
showing the meaning of 'work' to a wide range of social
classes. Its broad social canvas can be compared to many
novels of the same period.

Mrs Gaskell wrote two 'industrial' novels, both set in Manchester. The first, *Mary Barton: A Tale of Manchester Life*, was published in 1848, the year of revolutions (see page 4). Its eponymous heroine is the daughter of John Barton, a committed trade unionist and Chartist. The book is a study of the divide between rich mill-owners, symbolised by the Carson family, and poor mill-workers. In one section of the novel, John Barton and mill-worker George Wilson visit the poverty-stricken Davenports, whose main earner, Ben, has fallen ill with typhus. Mrs Gaskell based this description of the plight of the Davenports on scenes that she herself had witnessed:

> 'It was very dark inside. The window-panes, many of them, were broken and stuffed with rags, which was reason enough for the dusky light that pervaded the place even at midday... the smell was so foetid [nauseating, like decaying matter] as almost to knock the two men down. Quickly recovering themselves, as those inured to such things do, they began to penetrate the thick darkness of the place, and to see three or four little children rolling on the damp, nay wet brick floor, through which the stagnant, filthy moisture of the street oozed up...'

In a passage towards the end of the same chapter, Mrs Gaskell highlights the extreme difference between the living conditions of rich and poor. Wilson makes his way to the Carsons' home to seek permission to send Ben Davenport to an infirmary. Mrs Gaskell describes through his eyes the splendour and luxury of the mill-owner's house:

> 'Mr Carson's was a good house, and furnished with disregard to expense... As Wilson passed a window which a housemaid had thrown open, he saw pictures and gilding, at which he was tempted to stop and look; but then he thought it would not be respectful... he was ushered into a kitchen hung round with glittering tins, where a roaring fire burnt merrily... Meanwhile, the servants bustled to and fro... The cook broiled steaks, and the kitchen-maid toasted bread and boiled eggs.'

Mrs Gaskell was much criticised for her unsympathetic portrayal of the industrialist Mr Carson in *Mary Barton*. So in her second industrial novel, *North and South*, she incorporated a critical but more generous portrait of another mill-owner, Mr Thornton. The setting is again Manchester, thinly disguised as Milton-Northern, and a central theme the differences between 'masters and men' (one of the book's chapter headings). As its title implies, the novel also considers the differences between the north and south of England.

Hard Times

Charles Dickens (1812-70) set most of his works in London and his childhood home of Kent (see Biographical Glossary). However, one literary venture that took him beyond the southeast of England to the industrial north was Hard Times, the only work of his that is generally classified as an 'industrial novel' (see box). Dickens began to write the first chapters of the book in early 1854, and it was published weekly between April and August the same year.

Most of the action in Hard Times takes place in 'Coketown'. In preparation for writing his account of this mill-town, Dickens visited Preston in Lancashire, which was in the throes of a long-running strike by cotton-mill workers. Although the world of Hard Times is of course fictional, it owed much to what the novelist saw during his time there. Dickens's trip gave him the insight to tackle one of the main issues at the heart of the book – industrialisation and its effects – as well as the direct experience necessary to describe industrial scenes convincingly:

> 'It [Coketown] was a town of red brick, or of brick that would have been red if the smoke and ashes had allowed it; but, as matters stood it was a town of unnatural red and black like the painted face of a savage. It was a town of machinery and tall chimneys, out of which interminable serpents of smoke trailed themselves for ever and ever, and never got uncoiled. It had a

— THE SOCIAL PROBLEM NOVEL—

In his book Past and Present *(1844), the Scottish historian and essayist Thomas Carlyle (1795-1881) argued that industrial Britain could not be truly civilised or successful unless the huge inequalities between rich and poor were addressed. This idea, among others, gave rise to the 'social problem novel', also known as the 'Condition of England novel' and the 'industrial novel'. As these names make clear, such novels were concerned with the special difficulties of the times, such as factory conditions. They were a phenomenon particularly of the 1840s and 1850s.*

The politician Benjamin Disraeli (1804-81) was a notable author of social problem novels. In Sybil, or the Two Nations *(1845), he examined Chartist unrest (see page 10) among miners and handloom weavers in the north of England. He also suggested a solution to their plight, arguing that England could be regenerated by making the 'two nations' of aristocracy and ordinary people into 'one nation' again. In Disraeli's view, the loss of an old, natural, and co-operative alliance between these two unequal but essential parts of society had led to a large number of the ills afflicting the country.*

Many social problem novels made no specific suggestions about what ought to be done to solve the difficulties that they laid bare. Mrs Gaskell's Mary Barton *indicates strongly that the hardships endured by the working class people of Manchester are wrong, but ends only with a generalised plea for workers and employers to have more sympathy for each other. Most Victorian novelists were middle class and had little time for trade unions and militant workers' organisations. When trade unionists are portrayed – the activist Slackbridge in Charles Dickens's novel* Hard Times *is one example – they are clearly making the situation worse. Gradual reform based on mutual sympathy, co-operation, and understanding, not outright revolution, is normally the writers' preferred solution.*

black canal in it, and a river that ran purple with
ill-smelling dye, and vast piles of building full of
windows where there was a rattling and a trembling
all day long...'

Dickens dedicated *Hard Times* to the historian Thomas Carlyle
(see box page 23), whose reservations about the dehumanising
effects of industrialisation he shared. The novelist was also a bitter
opponent of Utilitarianism, a theory devised by the British philosopher
Jeremy Bentham (1748-1832) that was much in vogue during the
Victorian era. It taught that people should act in a way that led to the
'greatest good of the greatest number', but could be used to justify a
grimly practical approach to life that omitted any consideration of
individual personalities and emotions. *Hard Times* satirises this
approach to life as applied to both education and employment.

Like Mrs Gaskell, Dickens was concerned with the poor working
and living conditions endured by factory workers. But *Hard Times*
protests, too, at the whole industrial culture which, in the view of its
writer, forced people to work at a pace and in a manner that was
entirely contrary, and damaging, to their nature. Dickens mocks the
mill-owner Mr Bounderby as 'a man perfectly devoid of sentiment'
with 'a metallic laugh', and laments the tendency of his kind to
treat human workers like factory machines:

'So many hundred Hands [workers] in this Mill; so
many hundred horse Steam Power. It is known, to the
force of a single pound weight, what the engine will
do; but, not all the calculators of the National Debt
can tell me the capacity for good or evil, for love or
hatred, for patriotism or discontent, for the
decomposition of virtue into vice, or the reverse, at
any single moment in the soul of one of these its
quiet servants...'

In the downtrodden figure of mill-worker Stephen Blackpool,
Dickens portrays the deadening effects of factory work, which robs
men and women of control over their own lives. Shunned by
Bounderby as a troublemaker, Blackpool is also ostracised by trade
unionists whose strike he refuses to join. At this point in the novel,
Dickens also uses *Hard Times* to express his opinion not just of
industrialists, but also of union leaders such as Slackbridge (see
box page 23). In the novelist's view, they tried to force people to
conform almost as much as the factory-owners whom they affected
to despise.

William Frith,
The Railway Station (1862)

This is one of the best-known pictures of the Victorian age and is typical of it – people from a wide spectrum of society go about their business in the railway train, the great engineering triumph of the 19th century. It is also typical of much Victorian art in its conservative style.

Urban areas: the Midlands

During the Victorian period, large parts of the Midlands region of England became covered in urban sprawl. The 1871 census showed two Midlands counties, Staffordshire and Warwickshire, were among the five most urbanised in the nation. The reason was the area's plentiful reserves of iron and coal, found especially in the Black Country, northwest of Birmingham. Needed for building everything from railways to bridges, and for fuelling steam-powered machinery, these resources created great wealth for local business people and jobs for many thousands of workers.

The largest urban centre in the Midlands was Birmingham, a city whose importance had increased steadily from the start of the Industrial Revolution (see page 4). The opening of a new railway link to London in 1838 provided a further boost to Birmingham's prosperity. It allowed easier transportation of raw materials and other goods to the south than had been possible via the existing canal network, and made the city generally more accessible.

As in the north, urbanisation had a serious downside. Slums and their accompanying health and sanitation problems blighted Birmingham just as they did Manchester. However, Joseph Chamberlain (see page 14) introduced reforms that produced major improvements in his own city, and inspired similar developments in other urban areas. Chamberlain's achievements included the takeover of gas and water supplies by the city government, leading to better services, and the construction of Corporation Street (1875-82), a model road of houses and shops on the site of demolished slums. In 1879, a splendid new Council House (town hall) also opened. Its most noticeable feature was the 49m-high 'Big Brum' clock tower.

George Eliot

The Victorian novelist Mary Ann Evans (1819-80), who wrote under the male pseudonym George Eliot, is most closely associated with works set in the villages and provincial towns of the Midlands. As she was born near Nuneaton in Warwickshire, and often accompanied her father, a land agent, on his journeys around the countryside, this was a setting that she knew intimately. Against this backdrop, she depicted in detail the lives of a wide range of people, from aristocrats to agricultural workers.

Despite their mainly rural setting, none of Eliot's novels is completely untouched by the industrialisation, urbanisation and political reforms that affected 19th-century England. However only one, *Felix Holt, the Radical*, deals with these themes directly. This novel is set in the Midlands town of Treby Magna in North Loamshire. Eliot describes the profound changes, and particularly the industrialisation, that are affecting Treby:

'Treby Magna gradually passed from being simply a
respectable market-town – the heart of a great rural
district, where the trade was only such as had close
relations with the local landed interest – and took on
the more complex life brought by mines and
manufactures, which belong more directly to the great
circulating system of the nation than to the local
system to which they had been superadded...'

The main events of *Felix Holt* take place between September
1832 and May 1833, that is the period immediately surrounding
the 1832 Reform Act (see page 9). This legislation had both
increased the number of voters in elections by lowering the value of
property a man had to own before he could participate, and created
many new constituencies in industrial districts. Eliot depicts North
Loamshire as just such a district. The controversial election held in
Treby Magna to elect its MP forms the centrepiece of her book.

Even after 1832 most ordinary working men were still excluded
from the election process, and the novel depicts the attempts by
three Radicals of varying beliefs to win further electoral reforms: the
altruistic, morally upright Rufus Lyon, minister of a Nonconformist
church (see page 64), the worldly, unscrupulous Harry Transome,
Radical candidate in the North Loamshire election, and Felix Holt
himself. Holt is an idealistic young man who does not seek the
privileges of his middle-class status, but works as a watch-repairer
and tries to improve the lives of local miners through education. In
fact, despite the novel's title, he is not a typical Radical, as he does
not believe that giving all men the vote will of itself change society
for the better. Instead, in his view, all its members must strive to
educate themselves, and to act more justly, if the world is ever
to change:

'How can political freedom make us better, any more
than a religion we don't believe in, if people laugh and
wink when they see men abuse and defile it? And
while public opinion is what it is – while men have no
better beliefs about public duty – while corruption is
not felt to be a damning disgrace – while men are not
ashamed in Parliament and out of it to make public
questions which concern the welfare of millions a
mere screen for their own petty private ends – I say,
no fresh scheme of voting will much mend our
condition...'

In the North Loamshire election, which is the occasion of much
trickery and an ugly riot, the Radical candidate is defeated. In

reality, Radicals were successfully able to press the case for further electoral reform. As a result, a second Reform Act passed into law in 1867, the year after *Felix Holt* was published. It extended the franchise to some 938,000 more people, but the great majority remained without the vote. In the same year, *Felix Holt*'s publisher, John Blackwood, asked Eliot to comment on the new act through an 'Address to Working Men', written in the persona of Holt himself. In it, the novelist proclaimed her own belief in the merits of *gradual* change, which she shared with many other intelligent, well-read, middle-class Victorians. She also took the opportunity to call again for the establishment of a better world based not simply on electoral reform, but on higher morals and greater co-operation between different social groups:

> 'None of us are so ignorant as not to know that a society, a nation is held together...by the dependence of men on each other and the sense they have of a common interest in preventing injury. And we working men are, I think, of all classes the last that can afford to forget this; for if we did we should be much like sailors cutting away the timbers of our own ship to warm our grog with.'

Urban areas: London

In 1831, shortly before Queen Victoria came to the throne, the population of London was a little under two million. By 1871, it had reached almost four million, and by 1901 6.5 million. Many of London's new inhabitants came from the English countryside – experts estimate that about one third of 19th-century Londoners were born in rural areas. However, the city also attracted immigrants from other nations. By 1851, some 100,000 Irish people who had fled famine in their own land (see page 15) were living in areas such as Holborn and Southwark. In the 1880s, Jews escaping pogroms in Eastern Europe began to settle in Whitechapel and neighbouring parts of the East End.

Unlike the northern cities, London was not a place of large factories. On the contrary, the 1851 census showed that 86 per cent of manufacturers – for example, furniture-makers and leather-workers – employed 10 people or fewer. The growth of the city's working-class population fuelled the demand for cheap clothing, with the result that over the course of the 19th century, the garment industry became a major employer. By the 1880s, London's docks also provided jobs for up to 100,000 men. Their main task was to unload the cargoes of tea, sugar and other goods from across the British Empire (see page 17).

As in Manchester, so in London, the difference between rich and poor became increasingly marked during the Victorian era. But between rich and poor, another important group of people made its mark on London during the 19th century: the rising middle class. The men of this group usually filled low- and middle-ranking jobs in banks, insurance companies, stores and other businesses, working for example as book-keepers. Their great goal was to better themselves and their families through hard work, and their great fear to lose their jobs or to cease to be respectable. The middle classes aspired to live in terraced, or better still detached or semi-detached, houses in the suburbs, the new residential areas such as Barnet in the north and Croydon in the south that were springing up around the edges of London to accommodate the growing population.

The growth of London's suburbs was matched by the expansion of the capital's transport networks. The completion in 1836 of the first London railway, the London and Greenwich, marked the start of a railway-building frenzy. By the end of the century many thousands of passengers made the daily steam-train journey between suburb and centre. In 1873, one Londoner remarked that the railways had 'set us all [the middle classes] moving far away from London' and that only the 'upper ten thousand and the abject poor still live and sleep in the metropolis.'

London saw a boom in other forms of transport during this period, too. In 1863 the capital's first underground line, also the first in the world, opened between Paddington and Farringdon Street in the City. In 1890, the first electric-powered line was opened (previous underground trains had been steam-driven), and within 20 years much of the capital's present-day underground network was in place. Horse-drawn buses became a popular means of getting around at this time, too. By 1875, the London General Omnibus Company had nearly 50 million passengers a year. From the 1870s, trams carried many workers between their suburban homes and the City or West End. The original, horse-drawn vehicles were replaced by electric trams in the 1890s.

— THE DIARY OF A NOBODY —

One of the best ways to gain an impression of everyday middle-class life in the London of the 1890s is to read George and Weedon Grossmith's comic novel The Diary of a Nobody *(1892). The 'Nobody' of the title is the self-important and yet likeable Charles Pooter, and the diary charts his monotonous daily routine. Pooter's dream of middle-class domestic bliss is based on his house, with its 'nice little back garden which runs down to the railway':*

'After my work in the City, I like to be at home. What's the good of a home, if you are never in it? 'Home, Sweet Home', that's my motto... There is always something to be done: a tin-tack here, a Venetian blind to put straight... while Carrie [his wife] is not above putting a button on a shirt, mending a pillow-case, or practising the 'Sylvia Gavotte' on our new cottage piano.'

Pooter may be an exaggerated portrait, but in many ways he represents a side of life that most other Victorian novels do not reveal: one not tortured by conflicts between faith and doubt or religion and science, but concerned mainly with the minute personal details of everyday life.

29

Charles Dickens

The greatest chronicler of the urban scene in Victorian London was
undoubtedly Charles Dickens. One famous economist and journalist
of the period, Walter Bagehot (1826-77), perceptively declared that
'Dickens describes London like a special correspondent for
posterity'. Dickens spent much of his early life in Kent, but his
family moved to London in 1822 (see Biographical Glossary). Two
years later, Dickens's father was imprisoned in the capital's
Marshalsea Prison for debt. Dickens himself was sent to work in a
shoe-blacking (polish) factory on the north bank of the River
Thames. After the family finances improved, he returned briefly to
school, then moved on to become first a clerk in a solicitor's office,
next a freelance reporter in the law courts, and finally, in 1834, a
parliamentary reporter for *The Morning Chronicle* newspaper.

These early experiences opened Dickens's eyes to the two
contrasting sides of London life. The conditions that his family
suffered in the debtors' prison and that he himself endured in the
blacking factory left a lasting impression. Considering this period
later in life, the novelist wrote: 'How much I suffered it is beyond my
power to tell. No man's imagination can overstep the reality.' From
this time onwards, Dickens felt great sympathy for people who
found themselves in similar circumstances. However, his work in the
courts and parliament left him with a lifelong contempt for lawyers
and politicians.

By the 1830s, Dickens was learning more about London in
another way – by walking its streets and alleys day and night. This
was a habit that he continued for much of his life, exploring slums
and workhouses as well as middle-class areas. For this reason, he
was able to write convincingly about the capital's underclass and
bring stories about its members to a public that knew little of their
world.

Dickens's first literary work, *Sketches by Boz* (1836-7), showed
his skill for bringing London vividly to life. The sketches had
originally been written as newspaper and magazine articles, and
were intended to be '*Illustrative of Every-Day Life and Every-Day
People*' in the capital. In them, Dickens cast his eye over an
immense variety of characters, from pompous beadles to drunken
slum-dwellers, and portrayed in accurate detail the areas where
they lived. Here, for example, Dickens describes Seven Dials, a
notorious rookery (slum):

> 'The stranger who finds himself in 'The Dials' for the
> first time, and stands... at the entrance of seven
> obscure passages, uncertain which to take, will see
> enough around him to keep his curiosity and attention
> awake for no inconsiderable time. From the irregular

square into which he has plunged, the streets and
courts dart in all directions, until they are lost in the
unwholesome vapour which hangs over the house-
tops, and renders the dirty perspective uncertain and
confined; and lounging at every corner... are groups of
people, whose appearance and dwellings would fill
any mind but a regular Londoner's with
astonishment.'

Sketches by Boz proved to Dickens and his reading public that
London was an immensely rich source of material for creative work.
The novelist made his own fascination with the city clear when he
had one sketch character declare: 'What inexhaustible food for
speculation do the streets of London afford!'

As Dickens's career progressed – he was a full-time writer from
1836 – he was able to explore many more aspects of London in his
work. In *David Copperfield* (1849-50), his most autobiographical
novel, he translated the experiences of his own childhood and early
manhood into fictional form. There, for example, readers meet the
hapless but irrepressible Mr Micawber, who is modelled on
Dickens's own father and who, like him, spends some time in a
debtors' prison. They learn, too, about David Copperfield's
employment in a London warehouse, which is largely based on
Dickens's own time in the blacking factory (see page 30):

'Murdstone and Grinby's warehouse was at the water
side... it was the last house at the bottom of a narrow
street, curving down hill to the river, with some stairs
at the end, where people took boat. It was a crazy old
house with a wharf of its own, abutting on the water
when the tide was in, and on the mud when the tide
was out, and literally over-run with rats. Its panelled
rooms, discoloured with the dirt and smoke of a
hundred years, I dare say; the squeaking and scuffling
of the old grey rats down in the cellars; and the dirt
and rottenness of the place; are things, not of many
years ago, in my mind, but of the present instant.'

By the time he wrote *Bleak House* (1852-3), Dickens was
producing more complex works than ever before. Certainly the
narrative method of this lengthy tale, in which the story is told partly
in the third person and partly by one of the main characters, Esther
Summerson, is new. Dickens also shows a more developed ability
to consider not just a single issue but society as whole. Although
the main subject of *Bleak House* is the ineptitude of the legal
system, the author also targets the general corruption and

incompetence which seems to permeate every aspect of life, and which is symbolised by the fog that shrouds London at the opening of the novel:

'London. Michaelmas Term lately over, and the Lord Chancellor sitting in Lincoln's Inn Hall. Implacable November weather. As much mud in the streets, as if the waters had but newly retired from the face of the earth, and it would not be wonderful to meet a Megalosaurus, forty feet long or so, waddling like an elephantine lizard up Holborn Hill... Fog everywhere. Fog up the river, where it flows among green aits [islands] and meadows; fog down the river, where it rolls defiled among the tiers of shipping, and the waterside pollutions of a great (and dirty) city.'

Dickens's *Little Dorrit* (monthly parts, 1855-7) is woven from many narratives that form a complex picture of London society, two of which are the central focus of Dickens's attention: the Marshalsea Debtors' Prison, where his father and family had languished for some months, and the 'Circumlocution Office'. This fictional government department represents the Civil Service, which even as Dickens wrote was dealing with the Crimean War (see box page 16) in a shamefully inefficient way.

The little Dorrit of the title, Amy, is born in the Marshalsea, where her father has been imprisoned for many years. The hero of the novel, Arthur Clennam, attempts to help the Dorrits, but is blocked at every step of the way by the bureaucracy of the Circumlocution Office. Armed with the knowledge of government departments that he acquired while working as a parliamentary reporter, Dickens is well equipped to satirise this body:

——— DETECTIVE FICTION ———

In the early 19th century, many English people liked to read Newgate novels, romanticised tales of real-life rogues trapped by the criminal justice system. Gradually, however, tastes changed. As crime rose in the cities, organisations were established to combat the problem. They included London's Metropolitan Police (1829), which had its own six-member Detective Office from 1842, and a Criminal Investigation Department (CID) from 1878. Now writers turned their attention to detective work, and a new genre of fiction developed. Some of the earliest examples appeared in France, and also the USA, where Edgar Allen Poe's 'The Murders in the Rue Morgue' (1843) was popular. However, British novelists were not far behind.

Charles Dickens was concerned with crime throughout his career, and criminal investigations formed a major part of Bleak House *(see page 31),* Our Mutual Friend *(see page 33) and* Edwin Drood. *Dickens's contemporary Wilkie Collins (1824-89) produced what is usually thought of as the first 'detective novel',* The Moonstone, *and the use of detective elements in fiction grew steadily from then on. In 1887, the fictional detective Sherlock Holmes made his first appearance, when* A Study in Scarlet *by Sir Arthur Conan Doyle (1859-1930) was published. Holmes's logical solutions to Doyle's tightly-plotted mysteries set the pattern for much subsequent detective fiction. When the CID failed to solve the five terrible 'Jack the Ripper' murders that took place in the Whitechapel area of London's East End in 1888, Holmes's faultless sleuthing became even more popular. By 1893, Doyle was bored with the character and killed him off. However, public demand forced him to bring his most famous creation back to life in 1901.*

———————

'No public business of any kind could possibly be done at any time, without the acquiescence of the Circumlocution Office. Its finger was in the largest public pie, and in the smallest public tart. It was equally impossible to do the plainest right and to undo the plainest wrong, without the express authority of the Circumlocution Office. If another Gunpowder Plot had been discovered half an hour before the lighting of the match, nobody would have been justified in saving the parliament until there had been half a score of boards, half a bushel of minutes, several sacks of official memoranda, and a family-vault full of ungrammatical correspondence, on the part of the Circumlocution Office.'

Many of Dickens's works make reference to London's River Thames. But in his penultimate novel, *Our Mutual Friend* (monthly parts 1864-5), the river plays a central part and is also a powerful symbol of the city's filth and corruption. The complicated story revolves around an inheritance left by Mr Harmon, a man who has made his fortune from collecting rubbish, then sifting it for rags and other usable items. At the beginning of the novel, his son and heir John is apparently found drowned in the Thames by the dredgerman 'Gaffer' Hexam and his daughter Lizzie. This opening allows Dickens to introduce the river, which is covered with slime (in fact mostly sewage), and to make clear that it provided many poor Londoners with a living. When Lizzie protests that she does not like the Thames, her father replies:

'How can you be so thankless to your best friend, Lizzie? The very fire that warmed you when you were a babby, was picked out of the river alongside the coal barges. The very basket that you slept in, the tide washed ashore. The very rockers that I put it upon to make a cradle of it, I cut out of a piece of wood that drifted from some ship or another.'

— OTHER VIEWS OF LONDON —

Although the most well-known, Dickens was by no means the only author to write about life in 19th-century London. Others who made a smaller but significant contribution to the London literature of the period include Israel Zangwill (1864-1926), whose Children of the Ghetto *(1892) concerned itself with the Jewish East End, and Arthur Morrison (1863-1945), who dealt with the slum life of the area more generally in* A Child of the Jago *(1896). Yorkshire-born George Gissing (1857-1903) wrote about destitution in various urban areas. However, many of his novels are set in London, including the most famous,* New Grub Street *(1891). This novel deals with London's publishing industry and the way it stifled artistic integrity by making unreasonable demands of writers. Edwin Reardon, the novelist at the centre of the book, is forced by the system of publishing three-volume novels (see page 51) into a dreary life of overwork, producing 4000 words a day for meagre financial reward. Other characters, such as Marian Yule and Harold Biffen, are also victims of the system. Only Jasper Milvain, who churns out text with little concern for artistic ideals, succeeds in this mercenary world. He recognises that publishing is an industry like any other, and that to get ahead, a writer needs to give the public what they want. He is aware, too, why the others have failed: "'Both Reardon and Biffen were hopelessly unpractical. In such an admirable social order as ours, they were bound to go to the dogs"'.*

As the twists and turns of the plot continue, Dickens paints an ever darker picture of London. Corrupted by money, as symbolised by Harmon's 'dust' (rubbish) heaps, its rich inhabitants are shown enjoying themselves while thousands live in squalor alongside the river. Even once the plot is resolved – John Harmon reveals himself to be alive, and Lizzie Hexam marries happily – a feeling of pessimism about the future still hangs heavy over the book.

Urban improvements

As the Victorian era progressed, both city councils and central government in London made efforts to improve the lives of the urban poor. They were prompted not only by genuine concern, but also by complaints from the upper and middle classes. A terrible cholera epidemic in 1832 had led them to fear, with justification, that deadly diseases could easily spread from slums into their own, relatively clean neighbourhoods. The 1842 *Report on the Sanitary Condition of the Labouring Population*, by lawyer and campaigner Edwin Chadwick, spelled out the dangers. However, it was not until a second cholera outbreak killed about 53,000 people in 1848 that the government finally took action.

The 1848 Public Health Act set up a central Board of Health in London, with Chadwick as its secretary, and many local boards of health right across the country. Their main role was to clean up water supplies and improve sewage systems so that the careless disposal of waste could no longer spread disease. The system soon foundered, but many more Acts of Parliament intended to improve sanitation arrangements soon followed. These included numerous Burials Acts, designed to ensure the dead were properly interred.

— **DICKENS AND REFORM** —

As Dickens's career progressed, he became increasingly involved in active campaigns for social reform. One of his first major steps in this direction came in 1847 when, together with the rich philanthropist Angela Burdett Coutts, he set up a Home for Homeless Women. Most of these women were, in fact, prostitutes. Dickens continued his collaboration with Coutts for many years, for example also helping her to establish free 'ragged schools' for poor children.

Dickens was much concerned, too, with the poor sanitation in cities such as London, and with the cholera and other diseases that it helped to cause. He frequently addressed the issue in Household Words, *a weekly magazine of fiction and journalism that he founded in 1850. It contained a special section, 'Social, Sanitary and Municipal Progress', that included numerous articles on the subject, and so brought the debate to the general public. Dickens also befriended Sir Edwin Chadwick, whose 1834 Poor Law Amendment he abhorred, but whose contributions to the cause of sanitary reform, notably the 1848 Public Health Act (see main text), he much admired. Together with other like-minded campaigners, they were a formidable force for change.*

Dickens's other great interest was administrative reform. He was appalled by the government red tape that he satirised so expertly in his depiction of the Circumlocution Office (see page 32). He therefore readily joined the Administrative Reform Association founded in 1855, and made a major speech in its support. His commitment to the cause was also revealed in a letter of the time, where he wrote: 'I believe it to be impossible for England to hold her place in the world, or long be at rest within herself, unless the present system of mismanaging public affairs, and mis-spending the public money, be altogether changed.'

The problem of urban slums was one of the most intractable faced by Victorian politicians and philanthropists right across England. In the early part of the era, housing conditions for the poor grew steadily worse. This was especially true in central London, where large numbers of houses were knocked down to make way for railway lines, stations and grand buildings. During the course of the 19th century, some 120,000 Londoners lost their homes in this way. Lacking the money to move out to the suburbs, most were forced to live in ever more overcrowded conditions in the slum tenements that remained.

The British parliament moved only slowly to resolve the problem, and by the late 19th century the clamour for housing improvement was growing ever louder. This was partly as a result of new works such as *The Bitter Cry of Outcast London* (1883) by the Reverend Andrew Mearns, which exposed the depth of the slum problem in unsparing detail. One typical extract ran: 'Every room in these rotten and reeking tenements houses a family, often two. In one cellar a sanitary inspector reports finding a father, mother, three children, and four pigs!' A growing belief also developed that such overcrowded conditions were not only unhygienic but immoral, fostering all kinds of inappropriate sexual behaviour.

In 1890, the Housing of the Working Classes Act provided a new option by making it easier for local authorities to borrow money in order to construct housing for the poor. During the next decade, about 80 towns and cities took advantage of this arrangement. Yet still many people could not afford 'council housing'. For example, flats that London County Council built near the docks had rents far too high for most dockers. As the 17-volume *Life and Labour of the People of London* (1892-7) by Charles Booth made clear, more than 30 per cent of Londoners were still living in filthy hovels as the 20th century dawned.

3. COUNTRY LIFE

England's rural population shrank as its urban population exploded. Between 1851 and 1901, almost four million people left the countryside for the cities. But although the proportion of people who farmed for a living steadily fell (from 25 per cent in 1831 to just under 9 per cent in 1901), agriculture remained the single largest employer of men. The 1871 census, taken at the mid-point of Victoria's reign, showed that there were still 1,351,000 male agricultural workers in England.

Many writers, but particularly George Eliot and Thomas Hardy (1840-1928), created novels about the farms, towns and people of 19th-century rural England. Their works often look back with great nostalgia to earlier eras, but they also record the inexorable changes, from the mechanisation of agriculture to the arrival of the railways, that transformed the countryside during the Victorian period.

Landowners, tenants and labourers

Doctors, lawyers, businessmen and other members of the rising middle classes were all an important part of the Victorian rural scene, and featured strongly in many novels, including George Eliot's *Middlemarch* (1871-2). Yet throughout the period, it was the three main groups of people involved in farming – the landowners, tenant farmers and agricultural labourers – who formed the backbone of country life.

The wealthiest of the three farming groups were the landowners. They included aristocrats with huge estates and country squires with smaller holdings. In 1876, these landowners together numbered only about 4000 people, but controlled some 55 per cent of English territory. As the Victorian era progressed, newly rich businessmen who had made their fortunes in towns also bought land and country houses, or built their own country seats (see illustration opposite). At the lower end of the landowning scale, thousands owned much smaller pieces of ground, and did not enjoy anything like the prestige of their richer neighbours.

——— **EMIGRATION** ———

Many Victorian country-dwellers abandoned their homes not for the cities but for the other side of the world. Between 1861 and 1900 alone, about 755,000 people left the United Kingdom to begin new lives overseas. The USA was the most popular destination, but substantial numbers also made their way to Australia, New Zealand and South Africa (for much of the Victorian period all three were largely under British control). Many people felt these countries offered a far better future than Britain, where opportunity depended largely on social class and wealth.

This trend is reflected in Victorian literature. In Hardy's Jude the Obscure *(1895), Jude's wife, Arabella Donn, emigrates to Australia, saying: 'A woman of her sort would have more chance over there than in this stupid country.' Inhabitants of rural areas were not the only people drawn to new worlds. In Dickens's* David Copperfield *(see page 31), David's friend Wilkins Micawber also heads for Australia, proclaiming: 'I entertain the conviction... that it is, under existing circumstances, the land, the only land, for myself and family; and that something of an extraordinary nature will turn up on that shore.'*

Cragside (1870-c.85), Rothbury, Northumberland,
Richard Norman Shaw (architect)

The mansion was created for a wealthy arms manufacturer, Lord Armstrong, and combined the appearance of a gentleman's house which had grown up over the centuries (albeit in a style more typical of Sussex than Northumberland) with modern conveniences such as electric light.

Major landowners divided their acres into smaller areas that were run by tenant farmers – Farmer Boldwood in Hardy's *Far from the Madding Crowd* (1874) is an example. The tenant farmers in turn took on agricultural labourers to do the physical work in the fields. Hiring fairs were often held in the spring, particularly on the Christian religious festivals of Candlemas (2 February) and Lady Day (25 March). Many shepherds and other labourers with specialist skills were taken on for a year at a time. But thousands were hired only in busy seasons such as harvest, and on a daily basis. Then they worked for long hours. One Wiltshire man wrote: 'no one could stand the harvest-field as a reaper except he had been born to it. Their necks grew black. Their open chests were always bare, and flat, and stark. The breast bone was burned black, and their arms, tough as ash, seemed cased in leather.'

Although more Victorian women were employed in domestic service and manufacturing than farming, the 1871 census showed that a large number, some 85,000, worked in agriculture. Like men, they were often hired at fairs, and helped in the fields at harvest time. However, they also had other roles. Many, for example, worked as milkmaids, milking cows by hand twice a day. They also made butter and cheese in the farm dairy, as Tess does in Hardy's *Tess of the d'Urbervilles* (see box). Fruit-picking, weeding and the clearing of stones from recently ploughed fields were usually also tasks for women and girls.

As the hiring system was so haphazard, most ordinary agricultural labourers had no guarantee of work, moved from farm to farm, and earned very low wages. This was particularly true in south-western counties such as Dorset, where Hardy set many of his novels. There, tenant farmers did not

—— *TESS OF THE D'URBERVILLES* ——

Hardy's novel Tess of the d'Urbervilles *(1891) provides many insights into rural life and the economic and social upheavals that were taking place during the Victorian period. In fact, one critic, Arnold Kettle, has stated that the book has 'the quality of a social document... the thesis is that in the course of the nineteenth century the disintegration of the peasantry... had reached its tragic and final stage...'*

Hardy portrays his heroine, Tess, as a woman steeped in the history of Marlott, her home village, and completely in tune with her environment. For example, he shows her and other local women performing an age-old May Day dance that links them with village inhabitants of earlier times, underlining his belief in the importance of continuity and place in the formation of character. He also includes many scenes of traditional working life on Wessex farms, from reaping to butter-churning, as well as scenes showing the effects of modernisation on rural life. Until the mid-19th century, fresh milk was put in churns and transported from dairies to houses in the surrounding area by pony and trap. But from 1850, it was often taken to newly built railway stations, then transported by steam train to towns. When Tess takes milk to the railway station, Hardy makes clear the contrast between the naturalness of his heroine and the mechanical might of the train. Describing Tess standing near the locomotive, he writes: 'no object could have looked more foreign to the gleaming cranks and wheels than this unsophisticated girl'. This sense of dislocation is even clearer in Hardy's description of a steam threshing-machine at Flintcomb-Ash. It is portrayed as a terrifying monster, whose nameless engine-man is an alien presence among Wessex country people:

'He was in the agricultural world, but not of it. He served fire and smoke; these denizens of the fields [the farming people] served vegetation, weather, frost, and sun. He travelled with his engine from farm to farm, from county to county... The long strap which ran from the driving-wheel of his engine to the red thresher under the rick was the sole tie-line between agriculture and him.'

Sir George Clausen,
The Stone Pickers (1886-7)

Clausen was influenced by French paintings of
peasant life, although compared to French realists
like Jean-François Millet his rural workers (while
clearly drawn from real people) seem to inhabit a
rather softer environment.

have to compete with factories for workers, so could pay as little as they liked. A typical Dorset labourer earned about 14 shillings (just over £1) per week in 1900, while a Lancashire fieldhand could expect 22 shillings. To survive and avoid the workhouse, male agricultural labourers often relied on their wives and children to supplement the household income.

The housing available to farm workers varied widely. The most generous landowners provided tied cottages. They had to be vacated by the whole family if a householder lost his job or died, but were often well-built with good sanitation. However, many farm workers, like the Dagleys in George Eliot's novel *Middlemarch*, lived in mud-floored hovels. As thousands of agricultural labourers left for the towns, many landowners pulled down cottages rather than lease them to people not employed in agriculture, so making the shortage of decent rural housing worse. After farming was hit by depression, some landowners could no longer afford to build or repair workers' homes. As a result, the quality and quantity of rural housing deteriorated further.

Changing times

The years 1850 to 1870 are sometimes known as the Golden Age of English agriculture. Good weather, together with the increasing use of fertilisers, new land drainage techniques and more advanced agricultural machinery such as steam-reapers and ploughs, led to high levels of crop production. The repeal of the Corn Laws in 1846 (see page 11) led to a doubling of wheat imports during this 20-year period. However, English wheat farmers, who were concentrated in the south and east of the country, were still able to sell without difficulty all that they grew.

Farming fortunes began to change for the worse in 1870. As one wet summer

─────── *MIDDLEMARCH* ───────

George Eliot's novel Middlemarch *shows the many changes that the Victorian era brought to a fictional town in the rural Midlands based on the real town of Coventry. Electoral reform and the rise of the middle classes were among the most important. However, this complex book also concerns itself with the roles of landowners, farmers and agricultural labourers. The landowners represented include Sir James Chettam, a baronet who owns the great estate of Freshitt, and Mr Casaubon, whose large but gloomy home, Lowick Manor, 'had a small park, with a fine old oak here and there, and an avenue of limes towards the south-west front, with a sunk fence between park and pleasure-ground...' However, it is Mr Arthur Brooke, owner of a grand house called Tipton Grange, whose behaviour as a landowner is most closely examined. A keen advocate of political reform, Mr Brooke nevertheless allows his tenants to live in squalor, as his niece Dorothea points out:*

'Think of Kit Downes, uncle, who lives with his wife and seven children in a house with one sitting-room and one bed-room hardly larger than this table!—and those poor Dagleys, in their tumble-down farmhouse, where they live in the back kitchen and leave the other rooms to the rats!... I think we have no right to urge wider changes for good, until we have tried to alter the evils which lie under our own hands.'

In this novel, as in many others, Eliot was recalling an England that by the time of publication did not match most people's experience of life. As an article on Middlemarch *in the* Quarterly Review *of April 1873 perceptively noted: 'Somewhere, half in memory and half in fact, there lies for each of us a little country town, a Milby, a St Ogg's, a Middlemarch: such spots, surely, though no longer the representative and typical seats of English life, retain still immense general influence and importance; they are the haunts of our earliest and dearest reminiscences.'*

─────────────

followed another, the weather played its part. But far more damaging were the low-priced wheat imports that began to pour in from the USA, Canada and elsewhere. English producers could not compete, and the first of several periods of economic depression, together lasting until the mid-1890s, began. Many wheat farmers went bankrupt. Towards the end of the century, many sheep farmers went out of business, too, as cheap Australian wool began to arrive in England.

The livestock industry of England's northern and western counties was not hit so hard. This was because cheap wheat imports meant that the price of bread almost halved between 1870 and 1890, with the result that people had more money to spend on meat. In the late 19th century, the development of refrigeration led to rising imports of frozen meat, especially from Australia and New Zealand. However, many livestock farmers survived, as a significant number of English people favoured home-produced beef and lamb. Most fruit and vegetable farmers also managed to weather the economic storms, and many more people took up these occupations, planting crops and orchards near cities so that they could sell produce to the growing urban populations. Likewise, many failed wheat-growers turned themselves into dairy farmers, providing milk and cheese for city people.

Unionisation

Landowners and farmers were not the only people to suffer fluctuating fortunes as the 19th century progressed. Before the depression, wages for agricultural labourers gradually increased. Many labourers moved away from Dorset, Devon and other parts of the southwest where pay was at its lowest, often on their own initiative, but assisted migration schemes were also set up.

Over time, there was a fundamental change in the way labourers thought about themselves and the world around them. Men and women whose ancestors had known little of what happened outside their own village now began to learn much more about life beyond its borders. Trains made travel possible, and the new penny post (see box page 11) and newspapers brought news, including stories of unrest in industrial areas and of the unions that

—— THE ARRIVAL OF THE TRAIN ——

The construction of railways into the countryside brought the means of affordable and fast travel to many people for the first time. But the arrival of the train was greeted with much anxiety by many 19th-century agricultural workers who believed that the railway would destroy their way of life, and means of earning a living, for ever. Clashes with railway workers could therefore be extremely heated, as this extract from George Eliot's Middlemarch *shows:*

'Suddenly a noise roused his [Fred Vincy's] attention, and on the far side of a field on his left hand he could see six or seven men in smock-frocks with hay-forks in their hands making an offensive approach towards the four railway agents who were facing them... Fred... could not gallop up to the spot before the party in smock-frocks, whose work of turning the hay had not been too pressing after swallowing their mid-day beer, were driving the men in coats before them with their hay-forks...'

41

defended workers' rights.

As agricultural workers were thinly scattered across the countryside rather than crowded together in factories, it was difficult for them to combine in any sort of powerful trade organisation. If they wished to engage in political protest, they generally rioted, destroyed machinery or burned hay ricks, as George Eliot described in *Middlemarch*. From the 1860s, however, there were attempts to set up county-based unions, for example in Kent and Lincolnshire. But it was not until the following decade that a national union was established. This was largely thanks to one determined man, Warwickshire-born Joseph Arch (1826-1922).

Arch was employed as an agricultural labourer from the age of nine, working variously as a bird-scarer, hedger and ditcher. As an adult he also trained as a preacher in the Primitive Methodist church (see page 64), and became a trusted member of the local community. In 1872, following a request from a group of farm workers, Arch set up the National Agricultural Labourers' Union (NALU). By 1874 it had some 86,000 members, about 10 per cent of Britain's agricultural workforce. Arch himself was regarded as a hero in many parts of the country, and was celebrated in songs such as the following:

> Joe Arch he raised his voice,
> Twas for the working man,
> Then let us all rejoice and say
> We'll all be Union men.

From the mid-1870s, however, there was a backlash against the Union and its demands for better pay and conditions. Some farmers sacked NALU members or threw them out of tied cottages. Others replaced them with non-union labourers or with steam-driven combine harvesters and other machinery. NALU resisted farmers' attempts to break its power for months, but its membership was simply not large enough to stand up against them indefinitely. The depression of the 1870s weakened the union's position further, as reduced crop yields meant reduced need for labour. By the 1880s, NALU was in serious decline.

Despite this setback, the agricultural labourers who remained in work fared reasonably well during the depression

– 'THE DORSETSHIRE LABOURER' –

In 1883, Thomas Hardy wrote an essay called 'The Dorsetshire Labourer' for Longman's Magazine. It examined the effects of social change on the lives of labourers in Dorset, observing, for example, how the variety of traditional clothing had been replaced by uniform black, like any 'London crowd'. (Most now dressed in second-hand garments given to them by the gentry.) In Hardy's view, this made the labourers 'pictorially, less interesting than they used to be'.

In the same article, Hardy acknowledged openly, however, that a wish to preserve 'picturesqueness' should not be allowed to stand in the way of improving labourers' lives through education and other opportunities. In fact, he praised the new freedoms that labourers had won, and the trade unionist Joseph Arch (see main text), who had done so much to improve their lot. Nevertheless, Hardy expressed his sorrow at the loss of individuality that resulted from closer contact between different rural areas. He also made clear his greatest regret was that country people had 'lost touch with their environment'. It is precisely this link between character and environment that Hardy explored in many of his novels.

years. Wages generally remained steady or fell only a little, and thanks to cheap food imports families could buy more with their money. In addition, many labourers did not lose the new confidence that NALU membership had given them and began to expect more from their employers. Much as he lamented the waning of traditional rural life, Thomas Hardy recognised and welcomed this new mood (see box).

Electoral and land reform

During the 1880s, while the influence of agricultural unions faded, rural labourers gained another kind of political power. The two Reform Acts of 1832 and 1867 (see pages 9 and 14) had increased the number of men eligible to vote by thousands. Yet many people who earned only moderate incomes were still excluded from the electoral process. Arch and others campaigned to extend the franchise to these men, eventually winning the support of the Prime Minister William Gladstone and his Liberal government. Accordingly the Third Reform Act was passed in 1884, giving many agricultural labourers the vote. In 1885, Arch himself became the Liberal MP for Northwest Norfolk: the first agricultural labourer to be elected to parliament.

The 1880s also witnessed rising demands for land reform, that is the breaking up of country estates and their redistribution among ordinary people. This was not a new idea, but the impetus for change grew during this period because a series of Irish Land Acts had recently increased the power of tenants in Ireland at the expense of landowners. But despite a great deal of agitation by men such as former Birmingham mayor Joseph Chamberlain (see page 14), little changed. Some agricultural labourers acquired and farmed smallholdings – Chamberlain called for 'three acres and a cow' for every man who wanted them. However, by the end of the Victorian era, the bulk of England's territory remained firmly in the hands of the wealthy few.

THE YORKSHIRE MOORS

The Brontë sisters Charlotte (1816-55), Emily (1818-48) and Anne (1820-49) are associated with an area of the English countryside quite different from the rolling farm-lands that feature in the works of George Eliot and Thomas Hardy. The Yorkshire moors, whose windswept beauty remained largely unchanged during the Victorian era, were both their home and their constant inspiration.

The Brontë family moved to a village called Haworth on the edge of the moors in 1820 (see Biographical Glossary). Their parsonage home was surrounded by hills and uncultivated moorland, and the children spent long hours walking through this rugged terrain. The presence of the moors is most strongly felt in Emily's only work, Wuthering Heights *(1847). Of the three sisters, Emily was the most knowledgeable about the history, wildlife and natural features of the moors, and she incorporated elements of all three into her tale of the doomed but passionate love affair between Catherine Earnshaw and the handsome, tempestuous Heathcliff. The moorland location is central to every stage of the story. As children, Catherine and Heathcliff roam the moors around their home (called 'Wuthering Heights'), gradually deepening their kinship with this wild landscape and one another. After Catherine marries another man, Edgar Linton, she soon realises that she has betrayed her own nature and yearns not only for Heathcliff but the land-scape where he lives, claiming: 'I'm sure I should be myself were I once among the heather on those hills.' After Catherine dies, Heathcliff becomes convinced that her spirit is roaming the moors, calling for him. And when Heathcliff dies, the local people believe that he has joined her there.*

4. EDUCATION AND THE ARTS

During the first half of the Victorian period, the education received by English children varied widely according to class, income and gender. There were many different types of school, which all taught their own curricula with little government interference. In addition many rich children, especially girls, were taught at home by governesses, while the poorest often received no schooling whatsoever. The Education Act of 1870 (see page 48) set out to make elementary education available to all, and showed a new willingness on the part of government to deal with the issue. But inequality of opportunity remained widespread.

The schooling of both children and adults proved a fertile theme for many Victorian novelists, including Charles Dickens, the Brontë sisters, George Eliot and Thomas Hardy. The terrible conditions and teaching standards in some private schools, the difficulties of working as a governess, the frustration of girls denied the education that boys received as a right, and the struggle of working-class adults to improve themselves are just some of the subjects explored in their works.

Schools for the poor

Before 1870, children from poor families were taught basic skills such as reading and writing in a range of private, locally controlled schools. Few stayed on at school after the age of 13, and many, particularly the sons and daughters of agricultural labourers, ended their studies up to five years earlier when they began earning their livings alongside their parents. The poorest children went to establishments such as ragged schools (see box page 34) and dame schools. Elderly women ran dame schools in their

—— CHILDREN'S LITERATURE ——

The boundaries between children's and adult literature were ill-defined during the Victorian era. The most famous 'children's' books of the period, Alice's Adventures in Wonderland *(1865) and* Through the Looking-Glass *(1871), were written by Charles Dodgson, an Oxford University mathematician far better known by his pen name Lewis Carroll (1832-98). The books create a fantasy world with plenty to interest the mind of even the most intellectual adult.*

Many modern genres of children's literature were foreshadowed in Victorian times. Fantasy is represented by Carroll and by the 'nonsense' verse of the painter Edward Lear — The Owl and the Pussy-Cat *(1871) is the best-known example. There were school stories, such as Hughes's* Tom Brown's School Days *(see page 46); animal stories such as* Black Beauty *(1877) by Anna Sewell; historical romances such as Captain Frederick Marryat's* The Children of the New Forest *(1847), adventure stories such as R.M. Ballantyne's* The Coral Island *(1858), and combinations of the two such as Robert Louis Stevenson's* Treasure Island *(1883) and John Falkner's* Moonfleet *(1898). The style of children's fiction changed over the course of the 19th century. At the beginning, it was generally religious and morally improving, but by the end a secular tone was more common. There was also a distinct gender divide by 1900. 'Manly' adventure stories, often set in the colonies of the British Empire, were aimed at boys. George Henty (1832-1902) produced many such tales, including* With Clive in India *(1884) and* With Moore at Corunna *(1898). Domestic tales were aimed at girls, by writers such as Charlotte Yonge (1823-1901). Her works included* A Book of Golden Deeds *(1864). From 1851 to 1889, she was also editor of a children's magazine called* The Monthly Packet.

own homes, charging a modest weekly fee for what was often a basic level of instruction. Sunday schools, run by churches from the late 18th century, also became increasingly important centres of elementary education for the poor.

Religious groups ran many weekday schools that were either free or very cheap. In general, these establishments provided a better education than ragged or dame schools. Nevertheless, the standard of instruction was still rudimentary, as most teachers had no proper training, and in any case monitors – usually senior pupils – did much of the teaching. Despite these problems, each religious society ensured that the schools it operated taught Christian doctrines as it understood them.

Although by the mid-19th century many schools catered for poor children, thousands of boys and girls failed to attend. Experts estimate that in 1869, just before the Education Act passed into law, about 1.5 million children did not go to school at all. Like Fagin's gang in Charles Dickens's *Oliver Twist* (1838), many of them lived unrestrained and often criminal lives on the streets of large cities such as London.

Schools for the rich

Parents with enough money had a far wider range of schools to choose from, as they could send their children to fee-paying establishments. The quality of these institutions was extremely varied. Private schools at the lower end of the scale provided the children of tradesmen, clerks and others on a moderate income with a firm grasp of reading, writing and arithmetic before they left at about 14. Some of these schools were as grim as Dotheboys Hall in Dickens's *Nicholas Nickleby* (see box). But higher up the scale were the public schools, which offered boys from wealthy homes an education up to the age of 18 or 19.

Many public schools had developed from grammar schools that provided a free education based on the study of

—— **DOTHEBOYS HALL** ——

In Nicholas Nickleby *(published in serial form, 1838-9), Dickens turned his attention to the shocking conditions in a group of private schools known as the Yorkshire schools. Twenty of them had been founded in the 18th century near the Yorkshire town of Barnard Castle. Though all were a byword for incompetent teaching and ill-treatment, Victorian boys, many of them illegitimate, were nevertheless sent there. Dickens modelled the school in his novel on an establishment called Bowes Academy, which he visited before he set to work. The Academy was notorious because the parents of two children who had lost their sight thanks to an infection acquired at the school had fought and won a legal case against it in 1823. However, the school had not been closed down.*

In the novel, Dickens gives his Yorkshire school the name Dotheboys Hall. The book's hero, Nicholas Nickleby, goes there to teach after his father dies and leaves his entire family with no money. Dotheboys Hall is presided over by a cruel headmaster called Wackford Squeers, together with his equally vicious wife. When Nicholas sees the condition of the boys entrusted to their care, he is appalled:

'But the pupils—the young noblemen! How the last faint traces of hope, the remotest glimmering of any good to be derived from his efforts in this den, faded from the mind of Nicholas as he looked in dismay around! Pale and haggard faces, lank and bony figures, children with the countenances of old men... there was childhood with the light of its eye quenched, its beauty gone and its helplessness alone remaining...'

Latin grammar. However, the term 'public' is misleading, as by the 19th century they had become England's most exclusive schools, giving only a few free places to pupils who passed a scholarship exam. In the early Victorian era, Dr Thomas Arnold (1795-1842), father of the poet and critic Matthew Arnold (see page 70), began the process of revitalising the public schools. During his time as headmaster of Rugby School, (from 1828 to 1842), he introduced a new regime based on his own priorities: 'first, religious and moral principles; secondly, gentlemanly conduct; thirdly, intellectual ability'.

> ### THOMAS ARNOLD AND TOM BROWN
> *The novel* Tom Brown's School Days *(1857) by Thomas Hughes (1822-96) is set in Rugby School, where Hughes himself studied. The book charts the progress of Tom Brown from mischievous boyhood to brave and devoutly Christian manhood. At the same time, it is a hymn of praise to Rugby and to Hughes's old headmaster, Dr Thomas Arnold (see main text). Hughes's book emphasises the benefits of a healthy, physical life based on team sports and boxing, which is portrayed as the ideal way to cultivate manliness and sound moral values. For this reason, Hughes's fiction is often described as belonging to 'the muscular school'.*

As the Victorian era progressed, many new public schools were set up to join the ranks of long-established institutions such as Rugby, Eton and Harrow. Among them was Wellington in Berkshire, founded in 1853 in memory of the Duke of Wellington, a famous soldier and statesman who had died a year earlier. In both old and 19th-century establishments, children of the newly moneyed middle classes mingled with those of the aristocracy. Charles Dickens's son, for example, went to Eton, although the author had attended only a small private school. Nevertheless, public schools remained the domain of the privileged few.

Many of the grammar schools that remained free to pupils dated from Tudor times, and were still funded by endowments set up then. They offered a secondary-level education (to at least age 16) and were generally attended by boys from reasonably wealthy homes. From the middle of the century there were also some fee-paying schools for girls, for example North London Collegiate School (1850), and Cheltenham Ladies' College (1858). These establishments offered an academic education to girls. Elsewhere girls did study subjects such as history, languages and literature, but not in much depth. Miss Firniss's boarding school, for example, did not provide Maggie Tulliver, heroine of George Eliot's *The Mill on the Floss* (1860), with the serious education that she craved, and that her less intelligent brother Tom received from a private tutor. Girls concentrated instead on sewing, drawing and other activities considered suitable for wives-to-be. However, between 1871 and 1890, 70 more girls' schools were set up.

Some middle- and upper-class children were taught not at school, but by tutors and governesses at home – in 1851, there were some 25,000 governesses in England. Most governesses were unmarried middle-class women with little money, who turned to teaching as one of the few socially acceptable occupations open to them. (Factory work and domestic service as a maid were considered suitable only for working-class females.) The isolated existence of a governess as little more than a poorly paid household servant is depicted in many works of Victorian literature, notably *Jane Eyre* by Charlotte Brontë and *Agnes Grey* by Anne Brontë (see box).

STATE INTERVENTION

State intervention in educational matters began seriously in 1833, when the government introduced an annual school-building grant of £20,000. The Factory Act of 1833 also obliged factory-owners to provide two hours' schooling every day for 9- to 13-year-old children working in their establishments. This was the first compulsory education in Britain. In 1839, the government appointed the first school inspectors, and in 1853 introduced capitation grants (payment to schools of a fixed amount of money per pupil). A system of teacher training was also established – by 1860 there were 38 government-subsidised teacher training colleges. Schools that submitted to inspection could employ trained teachers that were partly paid for by the state, like Bradley Headstone in Charles Dickens's *Our Mutual Friend*.

As the 19th century continued, many influential people pressured the government to extend educational provision. Intellectuals and writers in particular worried about the problems caused by England's uneducated working class. Mrs Gaskell was in no doubt that John Barton, a

—— Governesses ——

The frustrations of the genteel life of a governess, educated yet with few opportunities, are tellingly described in Charlotte Brontë's novel Jane Eyre *(1847):*

'Women are supposed to be very calm generally: but women feel just as men feel; they need exercise for their faculties, and a field for their efforts as much as their brothers do; they suffer from too rigid a restraint, too absolute a stagnation, precisely as men would suffer; and it is narrow-minded in their more privileged fellow creatures to say that they ought to confine themselves to making puddings and knitting stockings, to playing on the piano and embroidering bags...'

Anne Brontë's novel Agnes Grey *(1847) also draws heavily on the author's own experiences as a governess. In fact, in the last pages of the book she claims to have compiled its pages from her diary. Both the fictional Agnes and the real Anne were equally unhappy in their employment, which Agnes describes as follows:*

'...a more arduous task than anyone can imagine, who has not felt something like the misery of being charged with the care and direction of a set of mischievous, turbulent rebels, whom his utmost exertions cannot bind to their duty...I can conceive few situations more harassing than that wherein, however you may long for success, however you may labour to fulfil your duty, your efforts are baffled and set at naught by those beneath you, and unjustly censured and misjudged by those above.'

When Agnes Grey *was published, one reviewer claimed that the writer 'must have bribed some governess very largely... to reveal... the secrets of her prison-house, or... must have devoted extraordinary powers of observation and discovery to the elucidation of the subject.'*

—————————

character in her novel *Mary Barton* (see page 22), was led into subversive Chartist ways by ignorance: 'No education had given him wisdom... He acted to the best of his judgement, but it was a widely-erring judgement.' The 1867 Reform Act (see page 14) increased the impetus for change. As it had created almost one million new electors, education seemed vital to enable them to vote responsibly. Industrialists were also anxious that their workers should keep pace with the educational achievements of those abroad. Only in this way, they believed, could British businesses remain competitive and profitable.

Many voices were, however, raised against increased state involvement in schooling. Nonconformists resisted strongly, fearing that if schools were run by the government, it would no longer be possible to teach their own beliefs in undiluted form. Some people worried that education would enable the poor to read revolutionary literature and so become more likely to rebel against their political masters. The rich were concerned that their taxes would have to rise considerably to cover the additional costs of running state schools.

The Liberal government led by Prime Minister William Gladstone was persuaded by the arguments in favour of creating a better-behaved, more productive and more politically literate working class. So in 1870, MP William Edward Forster introduced the Education Act in the House of Commons. Following many heated debates, it passed into law the same year. The Act set up School Boards in areas where there were not enough schools. The Boards then taxed local people to pay for new schools. Meanwhile, establishments run by religious societies continued and received money direct from the state. Elementary education became compulsory in 1880, when a new Act of Parliament obliged all children aged between five and 10 to attend school. The majority had to pay a few pence per week until 1891, when a further Act arranged for the payment of most fees by the government.

The 1870 Education Act led to the establishment of some 2500 'Board Schools' over the next 30 years. They did not

—————— *SELF-HELP* ——————

The Scotsman Samuel Smiles (1812-1904) was a prominent Radical and writer who during the 1840s gave a series of lectures to working men in Leeds about how to improve themselves. In 1859, he published a book called Self-Help *that was based on these talks. Smiles believed in giving more people the vote and in education for the working classes. However, he was opposed to state help for the poor. In his view, it was vital that they and everybody else become self-reliant and help themselves:*

> *The spirit of self-help is the root of all genuine growth in the individual... Help from without is often enfeebling in its effects, but help from within invariably invigorates.*

Smiles supported education to 'make the great mass of the people virtuous, intelligent, well-informed, and well-conducted', as he said in Leeds. Victorian novels often dealt with such self-improvement by working men. The carpenter hero of Eliot's Adam Bede *(1859), for example, goes to 'a great deal of trouble, and work in over-hours, to know what he knew over and above the secrets of his handicraft'.*

——————————

generally teach a wide-ranging curriculum or encourage independent thought – learning there, as in many other schools, was usually by rote. Nevertheless, the number of people able to read and write rose noticeably. In the 1840s, about 50 per cent of women and 67 per cent of men had to sign the marriage register with marks, but by 1900, about 97 per cent of both were literate enough to sign their names. Olly, a character in Thomas Hardy's novel *The Return of the Native* (1878), sums up the changing situation when he remarks: 'The class of folk that couldn't use to make a round O to save their bones from the pit can write their names now without a sputter of the pen, oftentimes without a single blot.'

Higher education

Until the 19th century, England had only two universities, the ancient foundations of Oxford and Cambridge. Students there were almost exclusively upper-class young men from public schools, and the classics (Latin and Greek) were the most important subjects. Both universities were closed to Nonconformists – it was necessary to be a member of the Church of England to join – and to women.

Change began in 1826, when University College, London was founded specifically for Nonconformists. As the century progressed, many growing industrial cities set up universities. Birmingham University, for example, was founded in 1900. The ancient universities were also obliged to reform. The first Nonconformists went to Oxford and Cambridge during the 1850s, and increasing numbers of students from rich middle-class homes were also able to attend. The first women's college at Cambridge, Girton, was set up in 1869, and the first at Oxford, Lady Margaret

─────── *JUDE THE OBSCURE* ───────

The central character in Hardy's Jude the Obscure, *Jude Fawley, is a stone-mason from the village of Marygreen with a passion for learning. Helped by the local schoolmaster, Richard Phillotson, he aims to secure himself a university place at Christminster (Oxford), and diligently studies Latin, Greek and many other texts. He also joins an Artisans' Mutual Improvement Society, one of the many educational organisations for working men that grew up in the Victorian era (see main text). In creating Jude's character, Hardy was inspired by a real inhabitant of Dorset, a teacher and archaeologist called William Barnes who managed to gain a Cambridge degree at the age of 46. The novelist's own exclusion from higher education by virtue only of his background was another spur.*

Jude's determination and enthusiasm lead nowhere. After moving to Christminster, he writes to several academics for help, but receives only one dispiriting reply:

'BIBLIOLL COLLEGE
Sir, – I have read your letter with interest; and judging from your description of yourself as a working-man, I venture to think that you will have a much better chance of success in life by remaining in your own sphere and sticking to your trade than by adopting any other course. That, therefore, is what I advise you to do. Yours faithfully,
T. TETUPHENAY
To Mr J. Fawley, Stone-mason'

Phillotson, who tries to win a Christminster place to train as a clergyman, is similarly disappointed, so both he and Jude have to abandon their dreams. In this way, Hardy demonstrates the likely fate of any ordinary man with limited money trying to gain a university education in Victorian England. Nevertheless, the novelist drew great satisfaction from the foundation in 1899 of a new college in Oxford specifically for working-class people. He believed that the establishment of Ruskin College, which is still flourishing, was due in no small measure to the publication of Jude the Obscure *four years earlier.*

─────────────

Hall, in 1878. But despite all these developments, most university places, especially at Oxford and Cambridge, were still filled by products of the public school system. Working men like Jude Fawley in Thomas Hardy's *Jude the Obscure* (see box page 49) had little chance of gaining admission. There were other possibilities for working-class men. They could participate in the university extension movement, which brought lecturers from Oxford and Cambridge to London's East End and other poor parts of the country. Or they could join organisations such as the Mechanics' Institutes, which offered a wide range of evening classes in technical and other subjects.

The publishing industry

The rising levels of education in general, and literacy in particular, provided huge new audiences for books of all kinds. The Victorian era was a boom time for publishing – some 40,000 new novels appeared during the period, together with countless works of non-fiction, from scientific tomes to religious tracts. By 1900, publishers were producing about 10,000 books each year. Demand was especially high at the cheaper end of the market, fuelled by a newly literate public.

People acquired books in a variety of ways. The richest simply bought them from shops. However, for a working-class person this was quite out of the question – a *good* working-class income was just 30 shillings a week, but a new novel cost 31 shillings and sixpence. Circulating libraries, which lent books to customers for a fee, therefore filled the gap. These institutions had existed since the 18th century, but became big business after 1842, when Charles Edward Mudie set up his 'Select Library'. By 1890, he had some 25,000 subscribers, and sent books all over the country as well as abroad. Mudie's nearest rival was W.H. Smith, but he had just 15,000 subscribers in the same year. Free borrowing from public libraries became possible after the Public Libraries Act of 1850, but by 1886, only about 100 such libraries had been set up.

The other main outlets for fiction were the bookstalls of W.H. Smith, which opened in stations run by the London and North-Western Railway from 1848. They proved a huge success, as many people facing long journeys wanted something absorbing to read. Small, board-bound 'railway novels' suitable for carrying in a coat pocket became popular purchases for travellers from the late 1840s. In the 1850s, they developed into 'yellowbacks', cheap books in

— BARBARIANS AND PHILISTINES —

Some people, particularly the poet, critic and school inspector Matthew Arnold (see page 70), voiced the opinion that the mass of people in the new, industrialised England no longer had any deep-rooted and unifying sense of culture. His book Culture and Anarchy *(1869), openly condemned the upper classes as 'Barbarians' and the middle classes as materialistic 'Philistines'. In Arnold's view, the only solution was to provide them with a more wide-ranging education designed to open both minds and hearts.*

_____

illustrated, yellow-board covers. Many were novels, but non-fiction books about topical subjects such as the Crimean War were also available.

For most of the Victorian era, until 1894 (see page 52), the preferred way of publishing a new novel was as a 'three-decker' (in three volumes). This was largely because of the circulating libraries. They charged people to take out one volume at a time, so gaining three payments for each novel and maximising their income. Publishers were happy with this system, as the libraries offered them a regular outlet for their wares. The quality of novels sometimes suffered as a result, however. Writers were often forced to 'pad' their prose in order to reach the required length for each volume, and to include cliff-hangers at the end of a volume to encourage readers to borrow the next instalment.

Many writers resented the stranglehold of the three-decker system. Chief among them was Charles Dickens, who therefore tried a different approach: serialisation followed by later publication in book form. The idea was not entirely new – sensational serials were already published in weekly parts for about a penny – but had never been tried for a middle-class audience. Dickens published many of his novels in 19 monthly 'numbers' at the price of a shilling, with the final, 20th instalment at two shillings. The format proved popular since it was affordable and gave people a complete novel for just 21 shillings. Dickens's best-selling work, *The Old Curiosity Shop* (1840-1), peaked at 100,000 copies per month. Writers who followed Dickens's example included William Makepeace Thackeray (1811-63), whose satirical novel *Vanity Fair* appeared in monthly parts from 1847 to 1848.

Dickens and other major writers also tried another option – serialising novels in literary or general magazines. These included *Blackwood's Edinburgh Review*, established in 1817. It published

--- C E N S O R S H I P ---

Respectable publishers tried to avoid producing books and magazines that might cause offence to the Victorian public, for example because of sexual references, and in this way they effectively became literary censors. However, the most influential censor of Victorian times was the library owner Charles Mudie (see main text). Works that Mudie banned, for example The Ordeal of Richard Feverel *(1859) by George Meredith (see page 56), often enjoyed little success. As a result, some novelists censored themselves in order to avoid a similar loss of sales. Others, however, were furious at Mudie's interference. In his pamphlet* Literature at Nurse, or Circulating Morals *(1885), the banned writer George Moore claimed that the librarian's 'motherly' behaviour was turning novelists into childish creatures too scared to express themselves freely.*

Censorship became less intrusive from the 1880s, and from the 1890s, the declining influence of the circulating libraries increased this trend. Hardy's Tess of the d'Urbervilles *(see box page 38) became the first important English novel to depict a woman who had had a sexual relationship outside marriage as a heroine. However, it provoked a scandal, just as* Jude the Obscure *did four years later.*

Some people, in particular a critic called Robert Buchanan, tried to censor Victorian poets, too. The main objects of Buchanan's anger were Dante Gabriel Rossetti and Algernon Swinburne (see pages 58 and 59). In 1871, he condemned their works as the 'Fleshly School of Poetry' because of their 'unwholesome' interest in the female body. But although Buchanan provoked much intense debate, few other critics shared his views.

---

some of George Eliot's early work, including her first novel *Scenes of Clerical Life* (1857), as well as literary reviews. Dickens founded his own magazine, *Household Words*, in 1850, and for nine years it published many novels in serial form, including *Hard Times* (see page 23). In 1859, the writer replaced it with *All the Year Round*, whose contributors included Wilkie Collins. The prestigious *Cornhill Magazine* was founded in 1860, under the editorship of William Thackeray. Among the works that first appeared in its pages were Hardy's *Far from the Madding Crowd*. As reading became more widespread and interest in literature increased, the number of magazines soared. Important new magazines of late Victorian times included *Strand* (1890).

    As the 19th century progressed, books gradually became less costly. There were many reasons for this development (see page 14). Book production grew cheaper as a result of new paper-making techniques and the introduction of more efficient printing presses. Publishers helped by reprinting successful novels shortly after first publication at greatly reduced cost. In 1852, the government outlawed attempts by the publishers to prevent booksellers from selling books at reduced prices. As a result of all these changes, circulating libraries gradually ceased to be as attractive, since readers could buy books at the libraries' subscription price or lower in the shops. Mudie and Smith began to lose money and responded in 1894 by proclaiming they would not pay publishers more than four shillings per volume, minus discount, for a new novel. This effectively excluded the costly 'three-deckers' and the format died out almost overnight.

Art

Much art of the early Victorian era was concerned with depicting scenes from everyday life or with telling a story, often with an improving moral theme. Among the main exponents of such paintings was W.P. Frith (1819-1909), whose works, including *The Railway Station* (1862) (see illustration page 25), were immensely popular. Some other Victorian painters, however, attempted to convey more complex ideas in their pictures, and expressed themselves through literature, too. Foremost among this group were the members of the Pre-Raphaelite Brotherhood (the PRB).

—— **WOMEN IN PUBLISHING** ——

During the Victorian era, many publishers and readers were reluctant to accept that women could be serious novelists. When Charlotte Brontë asked the poet Robert Southey (1774-1843) if she should pursue a literary career, he replied: 'Literature cannot be the business of a woman's life and it ought not to be. The more she is engaged in her proper duties, the less leisure will she have for it, even as an accomplishment and a recreation.' Faced with such prejudice, all three Brontë sisters published their first works (1847) under male pseudonyms — Anne as Acton Bell, Charlotte as Currer Bell, and Emily Brontë (1818-48) as Ellis Bell. Public pressure led to the revelation of their true identities the following year. The novelist Mary Ann Evans also used a male pseudonym. Even today, she is known as George Eliot.

John Everett Millais,
Lorenzo and Isabella (1849)

This was Millais's first picture to show the Pre-Raphaelite Brotherhood symbol PRB (in Isabella's chair). It illustrates a scene from Keats's poem 'Isabella, or the Pot of Basil', and Millais (only 20 at the time) used his friends as models for some of the figures.

The Pre-Raphaelite Brotherhood

The main members of the PRB were William Holman Hunt (1827-1910), Dante Gabriel Rossetti (1828-82), and Sir John Everett Millais (1829-96). Inspired by the writings of the the art critic John Ruskin (see box page 56) and the paintings of Ford Madox Brown (see illustration page 21), they and four others formed the Brotherhood in 1848. Its name refers to the Italian painter Raphael (1483-1520), who was often seen as a model of artistic perfection. The PRB, however, wanted to imitate painting from the 15th-century era before ('pre-') Raphael. In their view, this style was the most true to nature and went hand-in-hand with integrity of spirit. PRB paintings were detailed, with vivid colour, and people drawn from real models (Dante Gabriel Rossetti's sister, Christina, and his wife, Elizabeth Siddal, often appear – Siddal can be seen as Ophelia in Millais's painting on page 79). Many critics thought the Brotherhood's members arrogant for considering themselves 'better' than the great Raphael. However, Ruskin strongly defended them in his book *Pre-Raphaelitism* (1851).

The members of the PRB were always interested in literature, and in 1850 founded a periodical called *The Germ: Thoughts towards Nature in Poetry, Literature and Art*. Among the works that appeared in its pages were early poems by Dante Gabriel Rossetti. Much of Rossetti's verse was inspired by his wife, who died in 1862 after a miscarriage and drugs overdose. He buried the only complete manuscript of his poetry with her, but had it disinterred in 1869. It then became the basis of his collection *Poems* (1870).

Rossetti's poems are typical of the Pre-Raphaelites in being richly detailed, and containing the verbal equivalent of the paintings' colourful imagery. Rossetti also makes frequent use of symbolism drawn from medieval religious belief, and demonstrates a morbid fascination with death, or at least illness. Examples include *The House of Life* sequence of sonnets (1881), many of which deal with Elizabeth Siddal, and Rossetti's most famous poem, 'The Blessed Damozel' (1847, revised 1850, 1856 and 1870). The latter tells of the longing of a dead woman in heaven for her lover left behind on Earth:

> 'I wish that he were come to me
>   For he will come,' she said
> 'Have I not prayed in solemn heaven?
>   On earth, has he not prayed?
> Are not two prayers a perfect strength?
>   And shall I feel afraid?'

Rossetti created the painting that accompanies 'The Blessed Damozel', and that bears the same name, between 1875 and

Dante Gabriel Rossetti, *The Blessed Damozel* (1875-9)

Like Millais's *Lorenzo and Isabella* (see page 53), this painting unites poetry and art. Rossetti wrote the poem when he was 19, but later made two pictorial versions of it, catching his own combination of religion and eroticism well.

1879. It reproduces the poem's melancholy, romantic tone, and shows the lover languishing back on Earth in the panel at the bottom of the specially designed frame. There is a hazy, fluid quality about this painting that is not found in works by Millais (see pages 53 and 79) or Brown (see page 21). In fact, two separate currents of Pre-Raphaelitism developed: a 'realistic' tendency exemplified by Holman Hunt, (see illustration opposite), and a 'romantic' tendency, full of fantasy and self-conscious medievalism, exemplified by Rossetti. From the mid-1850s, the romantic tendency had a new exponent: Edward Burne-Jones (1833-98).

The later Pre-Raphaelites

Burne-Jones represented a new generation of artists and writers who came under the influence of the Pre-Raphaelite Brotherhood. He and others, such as the poet Algernon Swinburne (see page 59) and the poet, painter and designer William Morris (see box page 58), formed a link between this early Victorian movement and the late 19th-century artistic scene. After the death of Elizabeth Siddal, Dante Gabriel, his brother William, Swinburne and Morris all lived together in an artistic community at 16 Cheyne Walk in Chelsea, London together with, amongst others, the novelist George Meredith.

Meredith (1828-1909), the first to leave the community, is not an obviously 'Pre-Raphaelite' writer. His best-known works are *The Ordeal of Richard Feverel* (see box page 51), a novel that describes the successive relationships of an arrogant young man, and the sonnet sequence *Modern Love* (1862), which details the breakdown of a marriage. Both are more realistic than romantic. In fact, *Modern Love* brings poetry firmly into a contemporary middle-class setting, for example in the opening of number 17 where a couple keep the 'ghost' of their strained relationship hidden from their guests. The wife makes conversation, keeping 'The Topic over intellectual deeps/ In buoyancy afloat'. The guests see a happy couple, but according to

——— **MEDIEVALISM** ———

Medievalism — an interest in and attempt to reproduce the artistic styles and themes of the Middle Ages — was an important feature of much Victorian art. In fact, the trend started in the 18th century when many people began to look back with nostalgia to the medieval period. Different writers and artists were drawn to different aspects of the period. Some were inspired by legends such as the stories of King Arthur. Others made tales of warfare and romance the basis of their books and paintings. The influential Scottish novelist Sir Walter Scott (1771-1832) set one of his best-known works, Ivanhoe (1819), in the period of the Crusades, when knights fought for the Holy Land.

The main apologist for the Middle Ages in Victorian times was the art critic John Ruskin (1819-1900). In the five volumes of his Modern Painters (1843-60) and elsewhere he argued that medieval art was superior to that of any other era, a view that greatly influenced the Pre-Raphaelites in their choice of subjects for both poetry and paintings. The Victorian poet Alfred Tennyson also turned often to medieval themes, most notably in his collection of 12 long narrative poems, Idylls of the King (1859-85). These tell stories of King Arthur and indicate a retreat into a more secure past — a medievalised fantasy world of Tennyson's own creation. Medievalism also influenced Victorian architecture, and led to the construction of many new 'Gothic' buildings (see page 60).

———————

William Holman Hunt,
The Awakening Conscience (1854)

Hunt's pictures often convey a moral message; here a 'kept woman' realises the immorality of life with her lover. Every detail has some symbolic meaning, from the cat eating a bird (showing the woman's vulnerability) to the missing wedding ring (she has a ring on every other finger).

Meredith what they are really watching is 'Love's corpse-light shine'.

William Morris (1834-96) began his association with the Pre-Raphaelites at Oxford University. In addition to his artistic work, he wrote a great deal of poetry. He also published adaptations of Norse sagas in verse, such as *The Story of Sigurd the Volsung* (1876). He believed strongly in the political creed of socialism, as some of his later poems and particularly his prose fantasy *News from Nowhere* (1890) demonstrate.

Dante Gabriel Rossetti's sister, Christina (1830-94) was also a poet. She was a very devout High Anglican (see page 63); indeed her faith was so intense that it contributed to the breakdown of her two major love affairs. She split up with a founder member of the PRB, James Collinson, when he became a Roman Catholic, and with the scholar Charles Cayley in 1866 because she did not consider his style of Anglicanism sufficiently Christian. Her sonnet sequence 'Monna Innominata' (probably about 1880) expresses her emotional frustration and unhappiness. The 14 sonnets take as their starting point anonymous Italian poems written during the Renaissance. They told the story of a love affair entirely from the male perspective, but Rossetti gives the woman her own voice. In Victorian times this was a radical departure.

Rossetti's poems are often as religious as her own devout lifestyle. Despite being the work of a woman who increasingly led an invalid existence (see Biographical Glossary), there is a tremendous energy beneath the surface, especially in the flood of imagery. In the sonnet 'The World' (1854) for example, the world is personified as a femme fatale luring the unsuspecting soul away from the path of God. The description of the woman is strikingly grotesque; she is 'loathsome and foul with hideous leprosy', with 'subtle serpents' in her hair, and at night stands 'in all the naked horror of the truth' with horns and claws.

The Aesthetic movement

In the preface to his novel *Mademoiselle de Maupin* (1835-6), the French poet Théophile Gautier (1811-72) expressed a startling new idea: that the artist's only goal should be to create the beautiful. Beauty, he declared, is eternal, and 'the only truly beautiful things serve no purpose. Everything which is useful is ugly'. In this way, he

THE ARTS AND CRAFTS MOVEMENT

The influential 19th-century art critic John Ruskin preached the superiority of hand-made over machine-made artefacts, claiming that the true craftsman enjoyed an artistic freedom denied the factory-based worker. This idea inspired the Pre-Raphaelite poet William Morris, especially as it accorded with his own socialist view that art should be 'made by the people, and for the people, as a happiness to the maker and the user'. Having trained as an architect, then worked as a painter, Morris turned to the decorative arts, founding Morris and Co. in 1861. The company produced wallpapers, carpets and other furnishings by hand, and turned Morris into the leading light of the so-called Arts and Crafts movement. In 1891, Morris also founded the Kelmscott Press which began to produce beautiful hand-made books just as publishers were beginning to churn out cheap printed matter in earnest (see page 52).

initiated the cult of 'art for art's sake'. In 1873, the English scholar and art critic Walter Pater (1839-94) developed Gautier's idea in his book *Studies in the History of the Renaissance* which argued that art should not aim to deliver a political, social or religious message, nor indeed to achieve any practical end. Rather it should give 'nothing but the highest quality to... moments as they pass, and simply for those moments' sake.' Thanks largely to Pater, the idea of 'art for art's sake' began to circulate widely in England. It soon became the slogan of Aestheticism, the dominant artistic movement of the country in the late 19th century.

The English poet Algernon Charles Swinburne (1837-1909) was influenced by Gautier's ideas and attempted to put them into practice long before the 1880s when Aestheticism proper developed. For him, art was the key, and in art ordinary morality was no longer able to restrict the mind or body. Swinburne burst on to the literary scene with the verse drama *Atalanta in Calydon* (1865) and his book of *Poems and Ballads* (1866). The latter, with its tales of rape and murder, was seen as both shocking and excitingly rebellious. The sexual references are quite often explicit. Swinburne's early poems, in particular, arose out of his revolt against the institutions in which he was brought up. These included the Church, and his 'Hymn to Proserpine', which proclaims that the world 'has grown gray' as a result of Christianity, caused much offence. Thomas Hardy chose it 30 years later to be a favourite of the rebellious Sue Bridehead in *Jude the Obscure*.

Swinburne's poems are not simply the products of youthful posturing, however. His interest in alternative sexualities was part of a serious desire to use art as a means of breaking free from conventional morality. Swinburne's later poems often create images of harmony and unity, as if in art, division can be overcome. For example, in *Tristram of Lyonesse* (1882), when a famous couple of Celtic legend called Tristram and Iseult make love, it is:

'As though the world caught music and took fire
From the instant heart alone of their desire.'

Harmony is found in Art, in the harmony and music of verse, and Swinburne's is among the most musical of styles in all of English poetry.

Another writer whose exploits brought the Aesthetic Movement to public attention was the flamboyant novelist, poet and playwright Oscar Wilde (1854-1900). A renowned wit and *bon viveur*, Wilde lived much of his life according to Aesthetic principles, surrounding himself with beautiful objects and people but caring little for moral norms. During the 1880s and early 1890s, he became the highly fashionable author of comic plays (see page 78), children's stories such as *The Happy Prince* (1888), and literary reviews. However, from the mid-1890s, Wilde's work was affected by the decadence of that period, and his personal life was struck by tragedy (see Biographical Glossary).

The Aesthetic Movement also had important followers in the field of painting. Both Dante Gabriel Rossetti and Edward Burne-Jones accepted some Aesthetic ideals. However, it was the American-born, London-based artist James McNeill Whistler (1834-1903), a friend of Oscar Wilde, who adopted them most wholeheartedly. Some of Whistler's paintings were not of recognisable subjects, but rather arrangements of colours and shapes that he called *Nocturnes* or *Symphonies* (see illustration page 61). John Ruskin described one of these works, *Nocturne in Black and Gold*, as an 'ill-educated conceit' that was like 'flinging a pot of paint in the public's face.' Whistler sued him for his remarks, but won only a farthing's costs.

By the late 1880s, Aestheticism was shading into Decadence. This term was also borrowed from artists in France, and its practitioners aimed to set art free from the constraints of industrial society and materialism. Like Aesthetes, they mocked the suburban lives of the middle classes and sought to shock by their outrageous behaviour. However, their devotion to beauty was less strong, and a preference for images of corruption and decay developed. Decadent fiction in England was epitomised by a series of books called *Keynotes*, which had erotic illustrations by Aubrey Beardsley (1872-98). Beardsley also illustrated Wilde's controversial verse drama *Salome* (first English translation 1894), which was banned because of its depiction of Biblical characters (see page 78).

Architecture

Before the Victorian era, the dominant style of public building in Britain was Classical, based on the architecture of ancient Greece and Rome. After the 1830s, however, many different styles, originating from various places and periods, were all used. The most significant was Gothic, based on the pointed-arch style of northern Europe's great medieval cathedrals. The so-called Gothic Revival was in keeping with the general Victorian interest in the Middle Ages (see box page 56). Like writers, many architects looked back with nostalgia, believing that the Christian medieval style was somehow more natural and more moral than the controlled lines and proportions of pagan Classicism.

The effective manifesto of the Gothic Revival, at least in the early part of the Victorian era, was *Contrasts* (1836) by architect Augustus Welby Pugin (1812-52). The book illustrates the perceived superiority of medieval architecture with a series of pictures that compare a town in the Middle Ages and in modern

J.A.M. Whistler,
Nocturne in Blue and Gold: Old Battersea Bridge (1872-5)

Whistler, an American working in London, turned away – like the poets of the Aesthetic movement – from the heavy moral symbolism of much mid-Victorian painting to create pictures based mainly on mood and atmosphere.

times. John Ruskin later fuelled the demand for Gothic buildings with his books *The Seven Lamps of Architecture* (1849) and *The Stones of Venice* (3 volumes 1851-3). In both, he likewise emphasised the beauty, colourfulness and complexity of medieval architecture, particularly as seen in the Italian cities of Venice and Verona, and compared it favourably with the straight lines and plain, flat stones of Classicism.

Among the leading architects of the Gothic Revival were A.W. Pugin, Charles Barry, George Gilbert Scott and Alfred Waterhouse. A Roman Catholic convert, Pugin built many new churches, but is best remembered for the elaborate interiors of the Houses of Parliament. Charles Barry (1795-1860), was the architect of the parliament building itself; it took 30 years to construct, from 1837 to 1867. George Gilbert Scott (1811-78) was responsible for the Albert Memorial (see illustration page 13) and St Pancras Station hotel (1868-72) in London, as well as churches in many of Britain's towns and cities. The designs of Alfred Waterhouse (1830-1905) included Manchester town hall and the Natural History Museum in London. The works of many other Victorian Gothic architects, however, were at best uninspired and at worst downright ugly. Ruskin himself was appalled, calling such structures 'accursed Frankenstein monsters of, indirectly, my own making.'

Some Victorian buildings broke away completely from all previous styles and made use of newly available materials such as cast iron. They included the glass and metal Crystal Palace (1850-1), designed by architect Joseph Paxton (1801-65) for the Great Exhibition (see page 12), and the great Victorian railway stations, such as King's Cross, designed by Lewis Cubitt (1799-1883).

THOMAS HARDY AND ARCHITECTURE

Thomas Hardy trained as an architect and practised his profession in both Dorset and London (see Biographical Glossary). His particular skill was as a church restorer. Even after achieving success as a writer, Hardy maintained an active interest in his former art, becoming a member of The Architectural Association in 1862, and a fellow of The Institute of British Architects in 1920.

Hardy wrote many essays and papers on specialised aspects of architecture, but his architectural knowledge is also evident in his literary works. In Far from the Madding Crowd, *for example, he provides great detail about the houses of the major characters. Here is his description of Bathsheba Everdene's farm house:*

> *'By daylight, the bower of Oak's new-found mistress, Bathsheba Everdene, presented itself as a hoary building, of the early stage of Classic Renaissance. Fluted pilasters, worked from the solid stone, decorated its front, and above the roof chimneys were panelled or columnar, some coped gables with finials and like features still retaining traces of their Gothic extraction...'*

Hardy's professional eye is perhaps most apparent in Jude the Obscure, *since the central character is a stonemason. Hardy demonstrates his keen awareness of changing architectural styles, for example, when Jude begins to work in Christminster. The unwordly stonemason is still labouring under the impression that Gothic remains highly fashionable. But Sue Bridehead soon corrects him, proclaiming 'Gothic is barbaric art, after all. Pugin was wrong, and [Sir Christopher] Wren was right.'*

5. RELIGION AND SCIENCE

Christianity was an essential part of the fabric of Victorian society, yet as the 19th century progressed, the status of Christianity was seriously challenged. There were many reasons for this development, but among them was the rise of scientific theories such as evolution, which called into question the literal truth of the Bible.

Like the rest of the population, Victorian writers reacted in many different ways to religious and scientific developments. Some, such as the poets Alfred Tennyson and Gerard Manley Hopkins, clung to their Christian beliefs and continued to express them, however falteringly, in their works. Others, such as the poet Arthur Clough, became agnostics, claiming that it was impossible to know whether there was a God or what such a Supreme Being might be like. Still others, such as the novelists George Eliot and Thomas Hardy, abandoned Christianity altogether, and in their writings tried to work out the implications of a world without faith.

Victorian Christianity

Victorian Christians belonged to many denominations, often with sharply differing ideologies. The Church of England, the established (state-supported) Church, had most members – about 3.77 million were counted on a religious census day in 1851. However, it was itself divided between Low Church and High Church factions. Low Church Anglicans (Church of England members) were Protestants who believed that people could find salvation only through personal faith in Jesus Christ, and that the Bible was the ultimate source of authority. High Church Anglicans, by contrast, accepted many doctrines that were essentially Roman Catholic. For example, they believed in the importance of church ritual, and in the authority of bishops as well as the Bible.

Tension between the two Church of England factions existed before Victorian times, but was given additional impetus during the period by the rise of a new High Church grouping called the Oxford Movement. The Movement was led by three academics from Oxford University – John Henry Newman (1801-90), John Keble (1796-1866) and Edward Pusey (1800-82) – and set out to emphasise the Church of England's historic links with the Roman Catholic Church. Oxford Movement followers were commonly

——— RELIGIOUS TRACTS ———

Religious societies of the Victorian period produced a huge variety of cheap literature designed to educate people about Christianity. Most of these publications were 'tracts', that is pamphlets with strong moral messages, and the Religious Tract Society, founded in 1799, was one of the principal producers. Amongst its most successful publications was 'The Dairyman's Daughter' (1809) by Legh Richmond. This story of a farm girl saved from ruin by an Evangelical preacher sold more than two million copies. In 1879, alarmed by the lurid nature of boys' adventure stories, the Society began to produce a magazine called Boys' Own Paper. *It was a great success; the* Girls' Own Paper *followed in 1880.*

known as Anglo-Catholics, but were sometimes also called Tractarians because the group's leading figures explained their views in a series of publications called *Tracts for the Times* (1833-41).

Newman, the Oxford Movement's most prominent member, converted to Catholicism in 1845. He described and defended this move in his first novel, *Loss and Gain* (1847), but was still strongly criticised. As a result, he explained further in his much-admired autobiography *Apologia pro Vita Sua* (1864). Newman also wrote a great deal of religious poetry, including *The Dream of Gerontius* (1865). Its words, about a soul facing death, were set to music by the composer Edward Elgar in 1900, and used as the basis for the hymn *Praise to the Holiest in the Height*. Newman was made a cardinal in 1879 and continued to exert considerable spiritual influence until his death.

The Oxford Movement prompted members of the Low Church faction, often known as Evangelicals, to fight back. As the Anglo-Catholics introduced more ritual into services and sponsored the building of ornate churches, the Evangelicals promoted simple forms of worship and belief that had more in common with Nonconformist ideals. Few Evangelicals ventured into the literary world, however, as many doubted its morality. One exception was Dinah Mullock (1826-87), whose *John Halifax, Gentleman* (1857) tells the rags to riches tale of a young farm-hand. His success is achieved through perseverance and hard work – both virtues dear to the hearts of Evangelicals.

Nonconformists and Roman Catholics

Together the Nonconformist denominations (Presbyterians, Baptists, Methodists and other Protestants not allied to the Church of England) formed the second most numerous Christian grouping – some 3.15 million attended worship on the 1851 census day. As exemplified by the preacher Rufus Lyon in George Eliot's *Felix Holt, the Radical*,

—— ANTHONY TROLLOPE AND —— THE BARCHESTER NOVELS

Anthony Trollope (1815-82) was one of the most prolific Victorian writers, producing a total of 47 works. His novels deal with a variety of subjects, from religion to politics, and he also produced a range of non-fiction, including travel writing and a highly regarded Autobiography *(1883).*

Trollope's best-known works include 'The Barchester Chronicles', a series of six novels set in and around the imaginary cathedral city of Barchester. The writer was inspired to create them following a visit to the real cathedral city of Salisbury, and completed the first, The Warden, *in 1855. The second,* Barchester Towers, *followed in 1857, and the series ended with* The Last Chronicle of Barset *(1866-7). A principal theme of these novels is clerical in-fighting. As he shows clergy struggling to get their own way while trying to maintain an appearance of Christian charity, Trollope often exposes the bitter divisions between the Low and High Church factions of Anglicanism. In this extract from* Barchester Towers, *for example, the novelist explains how the newly arrived Low Church chaplain, Obadiah Slope, preaches a sermon designed to anger the High Church archdeacon, Dr Theophilus Grantly:*

'It is only necessary to say that the peculiar points insisted upon were exactly those which were most distasteful to the clergy of the diocese, and most averse to their practices and opinions; and that all those peculiar habits and privileges which have always been dear to high church priests... were ridiculed, abused, and anathematized...'

many were people with strict moral standards. They were often puritanical, too, for example refusing to drink alcohol, or to permit non-religious activities on Sundays. Many Anglicans found Nonconformists' fiercely held but rather gloomy beliefs hard to stomach, as an 1871 article in *The Times* newspaper explained: '[The Church of England] deals far more easily and comfortably with an ordinary man of average character... than the Nonconformists, who, according to their theology, try to persuade him that he is utterly lost, or graceless, or superstitious, or a fool.'

Nonconformists also faced direct legal discrimination. For much of the Victorian era, for example, they were excluded from Oxford and Cambridge universities (see page 49) as both students and lecturers. However, throughout the 19th century, they fought determinedly against their second-class status. The results were mixed. Campaigns to disestablish the Church of England, and so to remove its privileges, were a failure. However, non-Anglicans were permitted to attend Oxford and Cambridge from the 1850s, and the 1871 Universities Tests Act made it possible for them to take up teaching posts there, too.

The number of Roman Catholics was comparatively small – in 1851 there were probably some 900,000 in England and Wales together. (In Ireland, by contrast, Roman Catholics were in the majority – see page 14.) Since the 16th century, when King Henry VIII had rejected the authority of the pope and set up the Church of England, Catholics had been regarded with deep suspicion. Acts of Parliament during the 17th century excluded them from the army, parliament and many other important offices in public life. There were also severe restrictions on their rights to own property. The situation began to ease in the late 18th century, but fundamental change did not come until the early 19th century, shortly before Queen Victoria's

—— **A CATHOLIC CONVERT** ——

Gerard Manley Hopkins (1884-89) converted to Roman Catholicism at Oxford University in 1866, under the influence of John Henry Newman (see page 63), and two years later became a Jesuit priest. After his ordination as a priest, Hopkins set out to burn all of his early poems. Those that survive show his struggle to find a faith he could fully accept ('My prayers all meet a brazen heaven/And fail or scatter all away'). However, after he began writing again, in 1875, he was able to express his new-found beliefs through his work. 'God's Grandeur' (1877), for example, begins with the ringing declaration that 'The world is charged with the grandeur of God', goes on to voice Hopkins's view that the modern world is sordid ('All is seared with trade; bleared, smeared with toil'), then ends with a clear statement of his conviction that the beauty of nature is cause for faith, not doubt:

'And, for all this, nature is never spent;
  There lives the dearest freshness deep down things;
And though the last lights off the black West went
  Oh, morning, at the brown brink eastward, springs –
Because the Holy Ghost over the bent
  World broods with warm breast and with ah! bright wings.'

Hopkins did not, however, always feel strong and confident in his religious belief. In a group of later sonnets, the poet's despair at his inability to feel God's presence is clear. This extract, taken from the sonnet 'No worst, there is none', is typical of this darker mood (Comforter in this context means the Holy Spirit):

'No worst, there is none. Pitched past pitch of grief,
More pangs will, schooled at forepangs, wilder wring.
Comforter, where, where is your comforting.
Mary, mother of us, where is your relief?'

——————

6 5

reign began, when the Catholic Emancipation Act gave Catholics the right to hold public office and waived the necessity for MPs to take an oath denying the authority of the pope (see page 8).

Further important changes soon followed. Attracted by new job opportunities in cities, many Irish Catholics had been settling in England since the early 19th century. Their numbers increased greatly from the 1840s, as the potato famine (see page 15) drove thousands more away from home. By this time, the Oxford Movement's influence was also leading many English people to convert to Catholicism. Eventually, Pope Pius IX decided the growing Catholic population justified the re-establishment of a Church hierarchy in England. In 1850, he appointed Cardinal Nicholas Wiseman to the new Archbishopric of Westminster. Despite these developments, anti-Catholic prejudice remained widespread. Nevertheless, the so-called Catholic Revival prompted not only change in public life, but also a literary flowering among writers such as Newman and Hopkins (see box page 65).

Challenges to faith

There were many challenges to Christianity during the Victorian era. While leaders of the Oxford Movement encouraged a return to traditional faith, other clergy were taking a fresh look at the Bible. No longer accepting every word as divinely inspired, they began instead to point out contradictions in Biblical accounts, and to analyse the text as though it came from an ordinary book. Such questioning was not unusual by the mid-19th century, but in 1860 seven prominent Anglicans published a book that brought this new thinking to the general British public. The ideas expressed in *Essays and Reviews*, among them that the Biblical creation story was not literally true, provoked widespread outrage. Yet they seemed to tie in with scientific developments that were likewise fuelling uproar and causing growing religious doubt.

Charles Darwin (1809-82) was the Victorian who did most to cause science-based doubt. In 1831, he took a job as naturalist on a ship called HMS *Beagle*. The aim of the ship's voyage was to survey the coasts of South America, and Darwin made many careful observations,

– 'BISHOP BLOUGRAM'S APOLOGY' –

The poem 'Bishop Blougram's Apology' (1855) by Robert Browning (1812-89) shows the writer's awareness both of how scientific knowledge was undermining traditional Christianity, and of how people were adjusting to this new situation. The Roman Catholic bishop of the title, almost certainly based on Cardinal Wiseman (see main text), struggles to defend his beliefs to an agnostic reporter, accepting that faith has become harder:

*'Had I been born three hundred years ago
They'd say, "What's strange? Blougram of course believes,"
And, seventy years since, "Disbelieves of course".
But now, "He may believe; and yet, and yet,
How can he?"'*

Nevertheless, Blougram argues that God's existence has not been disproved *and that atheism is therefore as much a leap of faith as faith itself. The bishop is content simply to accept the inevitable uncertainties of life, to practise his religion in spite of his doubts and to live comfortably within the Church's social structure.*

———————

'This is the ape of form', colour print (1861)

The quotation comes from Shakespeare, but the real interest here is in the humorous and satirical depiction of Charles Darwin as a monkey. In a world before genetics, the assumed close relationship between man and ape was hard to comprehend.

particularly in the outlying Galápagos Islands. He also read widely, finding two books of particular interest. *Principles of Geology* (1830) by Charles Lyell (1797-1875) had already shocked many people. The Bible stated that God had taken six days to make the world. Theologians had calculated that this act of creation took place about 6000 years ago, but Lyell argued the Earth's rocks were far older. He also insisted that the Earth's landscape had been formed not in one fell swoop but by gradual processes such as erosion. Darwin had also read *Essay on the Principle of Population* (1798) by Thomas Malthus (1766-1834). It suggested the population increases at a rate that cannot be matched by food production. The number of people is therefore held naturally in check by war, disease and famine, all of which cause the weakest to die.

After returning to England in 1836, Darwin began to analyse all the information he had collected. More than 20 years later, in 1859, he published a book based on the results. Called *On the Origin of Species*, this historic work outlined a ground-breaking new theory: evolution. It stated that species of animals and plants were not unchanging, as the Biblical creation story implied. Rather they changed gradually over time, just as Lyell had suggested the Earth did. Darwin also argued that a process he called 'natural selection' favoured those changes that were most profitable to the organism concerned. To demonstrate this, he cited the example of different species of finch found on different parts of the Galápagos Islands. Each had evolved a different type of beak to cope with the particular food source (seeds, insects or plants) in its vicinity.

Many Christians found the theory of evolution incompatible with their idea of God as all-knowing Creator – why should a perfect God make something that was less than perfect and had to be changed? Nor was this the only problem. Darwin stated that while some species became better adapted to their surroundings, other species became extinct. This idea of 'survival of the fittest' was essentially what Malthus had outlined in his book – the most vulnerable creatures simply lost the battle for life. However, many Christians could not accept that the just and merciful God that they believed in could permit extinction.

People were quick to see the significance of Darwin's book. Within a year, in June 1860, a public debate was held at Oxford between Samuel Wilberforce, the Bishop of Oxford, and a staunch supporter of Darwin, Thomas Huxley (1825-95). Huxley won and Darwin's ideas spread further. In 1871, Darwin published another controversial book, *The Descent of Man*, in which he specifically discussed the evolution of humans from earlier forms of life. As before, many Christians refused to countenance Darwin's arguments, maintaining instead that God had created men and women as described in the Bible.

Darwin's ideas had a profound impact on the work of many major Victorian writers. Mrs Gaskell also included a thinly disguised portrait of the man himself in one of her novels. In *Wives and Daughters* (1866) the heroine, Molly Gibson, marries the local squire's second son, Roger Hamley. He eventually becomes a 'famous traveller' who makes important scientific discoveries in Africa. Some details are changed, but Gaskell's parallels with Darwin were deliberate.

'In Memoriam'

The struggle between religious doubt and religious faith was part of many Victorians' experience, and was nowhere more clearly reflected than in the poems of Alfred, Lord Tennyson (1809-92). Tennyson's career coincides more closely with the Victorian period than that of almost any other writer. As Poet Laureate from 1850 to his death, and as a member of the House of Lords from 1884, he was also a leading member of the Establishment. Nevertheless, he felt able to use his works not only to celebrate Christianity, belief in an after-life, and the idea of progress, but also openly to express the torment of doubt.

Tennyson was born in Lincolnshire, the son of a clergyman, and went on to study at Trinity College, Cambridge. In 1833, Arthur Hallam, Tennyson's close friend from university and the fiancé of his sister Emily, died suddenly on a trip to Vienna. Several of Tennyson's poems owe their existence directly to the period of self-questioning and religious doubt that followed this event, and deal with themes of loss, death and the after-life. 'Ulysses', for example, was written immediately after Tennyson heard that Hallam had died, though it was published only in 1842. The work is in the typically Victorian form of a dramatic monologue (an exploration of a single speaker's mind), in this case by the hero of *The Odyssey*, an epic poem by the ancient Greek writer Homer. In Tennyson's work, Ulysses is an old man dwelling on all he has lost, but finally realising that 'life must be fought out to the end'.

The chief product of the Hallam relationship and its abrupt end, however, was 'In Memoriam A.H.H.'. This poem, which brought

—— COMTE AND POSITIVISM ——

During the Victorian era, French philosopher Auguste Comte (1798-1857) developed a new branch of science. His aims were to further the scientific study of society and social change – what he was the first to call 'sociology' – and to develop 18th-century ideas that argued change was progressive and evolutionary, always moving towards something better. Comte wrote his greatest work, Course in Positive Philosophy, *from 1830 to 1842. In its six volumes, he argued that individual humans and human societies have passed through stages of belief, from religion at the beginning to science, what he called Positive thought, at the end. This idea influenced many British thinkers, including the political philosopher John Stuart Mill (1806-73) as well as George Eliot and Thomas Hardy.*

As time passed, Comte began to doubt his own ideas about the inevitability of progress. He also started to think that there was something important missing in his philosophy. In consequence, he invented a 'Religion of Humanity' that was similar to Catholicism in its principles but without God at its heart. The 'services' of this new religion were popular with British intellectuals in the mid-Victorian period, but by the 1890s the faith had only a few adherents left.

Tennyson real popularity and fame, was written between October 1833 (when Hallam died) and 1850, the year of its publication. It is in fact a series of poems in four-line stanzas, with an unclear storyline. Nevertheless, there is a dominant theme which mirrors that of 'Ulysses': progression from doubt and despair to faith and hope:

> 'If e'er when faith had fall'n asleep,
>   I heard a voice 'believe no more'
>   And heard an ever-breaking shore
> That tumbled in the Godless deep;
>
> A warmth within the breast would melt
>   The freezing reason's colder part,
>   And like a man in wrath the heart
> Stood up and answer'd 'I have felt.'
>
> No, like a child in doubt and fear:
>   But that blind clamour made me wise;
>   Then was I as a child that cries,
> But, crying, knows his father near;'

'In Memoriam' is notable in particular for its frank treatment of religious doubt caused by scientific developments. As the poem was published nine years before *On the Origin of Species* (see page 68), it was clearly not Darwin's ideas that led Tennyson to challenge traditional Christian belief. Instead he was influenced by earlier works such as *Principles of Geology* (see page 68). In addition to discussing the Earth's age, Lyell's book explained the views of French naturalist Jean Baptiste de Lamarck. Like Darwin, Lamarck argued that living creatures changed over time as features useful to them, such as a giraffe's long neck for reaching leaves, became more prominent. Lamarck's idea was also included in *Vestiges of the Natural History of Creation* (1844) by Robert Chambers. When Tennyson read a review of this book, he said: 'it seems to contain many speculations with which I have been familiar for years.'

Arnold and Clough

Two other poets came down firmly on the side of doubt in the Victorian faith-doubt controversy. Matthew Arnold (1822-88) was the son of the famous headmaster of Rugby School, Dr Thomas Arnold (see page 46), and both he and Arthur Hugh Clough (1819-61) attended the school.

In his famous poem 'Dover Beach' (1867), Arnold summed up his loss of religious certainty by using the sea as a metaphor for belief. In the poem he describes how the high tide of faith, when most people believed unquestioningly, has ebbed away:

'The Sea of Faith
Was once, too, at the full, and round earth's shore
Lay like the folds of a bright girdle furl'd.
But now I only hear
Its melancholy, long, withdrawing roar...'

Arnold is not trying to convert his readers to a new belief in Christianity, since he cannot believe its doctrines himself. However, he laments the loss of the reassurance that religion provides – without it, the world seems to have 'neither joy, nor love, nor light,/Nor certitude...', to be a grim and confusing place 'where ignorant armies clash by night.'

Arthur Clough, Arnold's close friend, is best-known for a short satirical poem, 'The Latest Decalogue'. In it, he reworks the Biblical Ten Commandments to suit bourgeois society in the mid-19th century, with its hypocrisies and obsession with profit:

'Honour thy parents; that is, all
From whom advancement may befall . . .
Thou shalt not steal; an empty feat,
When it's so lucrative to cheat.'

This is typical of both Clough's and Arnold's work in that it considers serious matters with a hint of wit. In many of his other poems, however, Clough agonises over his doubts about religious belief. One of these 'doubt' poems bears the Italian title 'Perchè pensa? Pensando s'invecchia'. This means 'Why think? While you think you get old', and the works shows Clough's impatience at never being able to understand 'the purpose of our being here'. Clough's continual inconclusive revisiting of the arguments for faith and doubt often leads to a feeling of stalemate. 'Easter Day' consists of a long section with the refrain 'Christ is not risen!' and a short tailpiece in which a voice sings a different chorus in Clough's ear:

'In the true Creed
He is yet risen indeed;
        Christ is yet risen.'

Crucially, however, there is no real sense that Clough has accepted this voice of faith, even if he allows it to finish his poem.

Brave clearness and honesty'

Novelists were affected just as much by the religious uncertainties of Victorian times as poets. George Eliot was a case in point. Brought up as an Anglican, she was deeply influenced by the piety of a strict

Methodist aunt and the Nonconformist ministers who ran the schools she attended. However, after her enthusiasm for religious matters led her to begin a close study of church history, Eliot was utterly disillusioned by the record of in-fighting and brutality that she uncovered. At about the same time, she became interested in thinkers who sought to explain the world by rational means. They included the Scot David Hume (1711-76) and other 18th- and 19th-century philosophers who suggested that God could not exist, or did not need to.

People whom Eliot knew personally now began to add to her doubts. Among them was Charles Bray, a supporter of the industrialist Robert Owen. Owen was famous especially for having built a model village for his workers in New Lanark near Glasgow. However, he had completely rejected conventional religion and Bray had done likewise. Eliot's brother-in-law, Charles Hennell, was another man whose views chipped away at the foundations of her faith. He had written a book called *Inquiry Concerning the Origins of Christianity* (1838) that reinforced all her own findings about the dubious nature of much church history. By the 1840s, Eliot had become convinced that God did not exist and in early 1842 refused to go to church with her father, Robert. Four years later, she translated from German *Das Leben Jesu* (*The Life of Jesus*) by David Friedrich Strauss. This work views Christ as a strictly historical figure rather than the Son of God, and influenced many liberal theologians in England.

The growing scientific causes of religious doubt were not a major factor in Eliot's loss of faith, which occurred long before Darwin's *On the Origin of Species* appeared in 1859. By that time, she was already familiar with the notion that living things had developed over time, as it had been suggested in outline by some earlier scientists (see page 70). In fact, she considered Darwin's book 'ill-written and sadly wanting in illustrative facts', but nevertheless commended him for his long years of study and for bringing the world a step closer to 'brave clearness and honesty'.

Despite her eventual lack of belief, Eliot constantly engaged with religious themes in her works – indeed her first published book was a series of three short novels called *Scenes of Clerical Life*. Frequently, she exposes the hypocrisy at the heart of much religion. In *The Mill on the Floss*, for example, Eliot carefully demonstrates that the beliefs of the people of St Ogg's bear little relation to the moral principles taught by the Christian church: 'Observing these people narrowly... one sees little trace of religion, still less of a distinctively Christian creed. Their belief in the unseen, so far as it manifests itself at all, seems to be rather of a pagan kind: their moral notions, though held with strong tenacity, seem to have no standard beyond hereditary custom.'

'The Cathedral has had its day!'

Thomas Hardy was brought up as a High Church Anglican, and like Eliot was for many years a firm believer – as a child his ambition was to be ordained a Christian minister. As an architect, Hardy spent much of his time renovating churches, work that he loved. Yet despite this firm grounding in belief and tradition, he slowly lost his faith.

The scientific work of Lyell and Darwin (see page 68) was a major factor in Hardy's falling away from religious belief. Lyell's books convinced Hardy that humanity was relatively insignificant when set against the great natural forces that had shaped the Earth over millions of years. A scene from his early novel *A Pair of Blue Eyes* (1873) brings this powerfully home. When one of the main characters, Charles Knight, falls off a cliff and is clinging on to life by his fingertips, he comes face to face with the fossil of an ancient sea creature called a trilobite. In so doing, Knight realises that he will die just as the trilobite had done, and that both events have little meaning in the great scheme of evolution:

> 'Separated by millions of years in their lives, Knight and this underling seemed to have met in their place of death. It was the single instance within reach of his vision of anything that had ever been alive and had had a body to save, as he himself had now.'

In his writings, Darwin expressed in scientific terms what Hardy had already begun to notice as a child – that nature had no morality, that God did not step in to protect the weakest of his creatures, that in other words it was the fittest who survived. Such ideas are deeply embedded in Hardy's poetry as well as his novels.

Hardy's unbelief, or at best agnosticism, was fostered by non-scientific thinkers, too. Among them was Thomas Huxley, a close associate and great defender of Darwin (see page 68). Huxley coined the term 'agnosticism' for the conviction that the existence or non-existence of a God cannot be proved or deduced in any rational way. Hardy examined this viewpoint in his poem 'The Impercipient' (published 1898). Unlike the people around him, what

---

—— TALES OF THE SUPERNATURAL ——

The Victorians' interest in the supernatural was not limited to the realm of traditional religion. Stories about ghosts, vampires and other mysterious creatures were hugely popular. These tales were descended from the 'Gothic' fiction of the late 18th and early 19th century, which likewise featured supernatural events – the most well-known Gothic novel is Mary Shelley's Frankenstein *(1818). Ghost stories were widely read throughout the 19th century – Dickens's* A Christmas Carol *(1843), the tale of the miser Scrooge's conversion to Christian charity through ghostly intervention, is probably the most famous example. Other outstanding supernatural novels of the late Victorian period were not strictly ghost stories.* The Strange Case of Dr Jekyll and Mr Hyde *(1886) by the Scottish writer Robert Louis Stevenson (1850-94), relates how Dr Jekyll manufactures a drug that allows him to turn the evil side of himself into a separate person, Mr Hyde.* Dracula *(1897) by the Irish writer Bram Stoker (1847-1912), is a spine-chilling tale of vampires.*

---

he – 'the impercipient' of the title – cannot perceive is the sea that they can all hear. Instead, he makes the rational assumption that it is simply a pine tree rustling in the wind:

> I am like a gazer who should mark
>> An inland company
> Standing upfingered, with, 'Hark! hark!
>> The glorious distant sea!'
> And feel, 'Alas, 'tis but yon dark
>> And wind-swept pine to me!'

The sea in the poem is a metaphor for the God that Hardy cannot perceive, but rather explains away with rational argument. Agnosticism or sometimes out-and-out atheism is also the declared creed of several major characters in Hardy's novels. Among them is Sue Bridehead, the unconventional heroine of *Jude the Obscure*. She proclaims that she would rather sit in the railway station than in Melchester Cathedral, because 'The Cathedral has had its day!'.

Hardy's traditional religious faith was gradually replaced by two new strands of thought, one pessimistic, the other optimistic. The novelist became convinced that humans were at the mercy of blind chance and that sheer coincidence could ruin people's lives forever. Such concidences are often used as a plot device in Hardy's novels. Hardy's more optimistic beliefs were shaped by the Positivist ideas of Auguste Comte (see box page 69). Hardy believed, with Comte, that flawed humanity rather than a perfect but probably imaginary God should be an object of worship. He put Positivist words into the mouths of characters such as Clym Yeobright in *The Return of the Native* and Angel Clare in *Tess of the d'Urbervilles*. He also expressed his Positivist convictions in his 1914 poem 'A Plaint to Man', which is written as though by God addressing humanity:

> And now that I dwindle day by day
> Beneath the deicide eyes of seers
> In a light that will not let me stay
>
> And tomorrow the whole of me disappears,
> The truth should be told and the fact be faced
> That had best been faced in earlier years:
>
> The fact of life with dependence placed
> On the human heart's resource alone,
> In brotherhood bonded close and graced
>
> With loving-kindness fully blown,
> And visioned help, unsought, unknown.

6.VICTORIAN DRAMA

The Victorian era is usually seen as an age of fiction, and to a lesser extent poetry, but it would be wrong to dismiss the drama of the period entirely. The earlier drama is now more easily found in print and has seen a modest revival in the theatre, while some major writers were active towards the end of the period.

In the earlier Victorian period it is noticeable that few major novelists also wrote plays. Some poets were also playwrights, but on the whole their dramas are not well known. One reason may well be the fact that plays were simply not as profitable as fiction. One of the main dramatists of the earlier part of the period, Tom Taylor, received a one-off payment of only £200 for his play *The Ticket-of-Leave Man*, which was a major popular success. The dramatically conceived novels of Dickens were known on the stage, but only through very successful adaptations by others. Their serial publication (see page 51) resulted in frequent dramatic climaxes (at the end of a monthly instalment for example) which transferred well to the stage.

French influence was strong. In particular, the dramatic practice of Eugène Scribe (1791-1861) affected melodrama, social drama and comedy – the three main currents in the Victorian theatre. Scribe wrote some 300 plays, often in collaboration, and is mainly known for the *pièce bien faite* or 'well-made play', in which plotting is complex but tight and well-planned, with one scene leading logically to the next. It was important for the tension to increase throughout in order to build up to the revelations in a *scène à faire*, the 'scene which must be written'. This could all seem artificial and unrealistic, but used the time-dependent medium of the theatre to good effect, producing satisfying endings and guaranteeing coherent plays with a clear purpose. Many later dramatists owed Scribe a debt, even if they officially opposed the idea of the *pièce bien faite*.

—— THEATRES ——

Victorian theatres were often large – Covent Garden and Drury Lane both held audiences of 3000 or more. The number of theatres increased throughout the century: London had more than 20 by 1850 and more than 60 by 1900 (not including music halls). Technological developments included changes in lighting which enabled the audience to sit in darkness during the performance (from 1849) and the introduction of electric light (1881). Electricity was safer than previous forms of lighting such as candles, oil-lamps, gaslight and limelight, and was easier to control, although beautiful effects were possible with limelight.

The Victorian theatre-going public expected to be entertained visually by the play itself. Sometimes playscripts called for a 'tableau', rather like a 'freeze frame' in video, in which the actors stood still in attitudes expressing the moral or dramatic point of a particular scene. The lighting and the sets also became extremely elaborate, especially for melodrama. Douglas Jerrold's Black-Ey'd Susan *(see page 76) is typical in requiring a whole series of detailed and painstakingly painted backcloths, with views of the country, of the town of Deal, and of the sea with ships at anchor. When (in Act 1 Scene 1) Doggrass and Gnatbrain refer to a milestone, a fire, and the 'trees growing about us', a Victorian audience expected to see realistic versions of these items on the stage. Later plays required even more: Act II Scene 6 of Irish playwright Dion Boucicault's* The Colleen Bawn *(1860), for example, calls for a cave, a lake, the moon, rocks and 'gauze waters all over stage' which were made to look stormy by placing small boys underneath to move the gauze waves up and down.*

Melodrama

Melodrama was the dominant style of this time. It appealed to a wide range of social classes with its mixture of highly dramatic situations, heightened emotions, and convenient conventions (the pure, innocent heroine was always in white, for example). Dickens's public readings, which he began in December 1853, showed some features of melodrama in often being comic, sentimental or (in the case of the 'Sikes and Nancy' episode from *Oliver Twist*) horrific. It is also interesting that they attracted a sizeable working-class following, to a certain extent bridging the gap between popular and middle-class culture. John Forster, Dickens's first biographer, was in no doubt that the public readings were undignified and unworthy of a gentleman.

Other features of melodrama (not used in Dickens's readings) included elaborate scenery and music, which was used throughout to manipulate the audience's emotions – a practice later transferred to silent films. A typical and extremely popular example of a melodrama was Douglas Jerrold's *Black-Ey'd Susan* (1829). This play takes its audience through rapid changes of emotion (fear, terror, joy and patriotic pride) with music, dancing and spectacular scenery including ships and a smugglers' cave. Dickens found it 'fresh and vigorous... manly and gallant', and it was regularly performed until 1897. Part of the end of Act II gives a flavour of the style, as well as of the highly stylised roles played by hero and heroine and the obvious moral messages for the audience:

> **Captain Crosslee:** Passion hurries me – the wine fires me – your eyes dart lightning into me, and you shall be mine! [Seizes Susan.]
> **Susan:** Let me go! in mercy! – William, William!
> **Crosslee:** Your cries are vain! resistance useless!
> **Susan:** Monster! William, William!
> [William rushes in L., with his drawn cutlass]
> **William:** Susan! and attacked by the buccaneers! die!
> [William strikes at the CAPTAIN, whose back is turned towards him – he falls.]
> **Crosslee:** I deserve my fate.

——— VICTORIAN MUSIC ———

In continental Europe, Victorian England was known as 'the land without music', since it produced no major classical composers to rival artists such as the Czech Antonin Dvořák (1841-1904) or the Frenchman Gabriel Fauré (1845-1924). The most gifted English composer of the period, in fact an Anglo-Irishman, was Charles Villiers Stanford (1852-1924). He was known especially for his operas and choral works, but his main influence was as a teacher at the Royal College of Music. Despite this weakness, other forms of music flourished during the Victorian era. During the 1840s, a man called John Curwen invented the tonic sol-fa system, which made it possible to learn scales by singing syllables rather than reading notes on a stave. As a result, musical understanding spread rapidly, and many amateur choirs were formed. Many people liked to hold musical evenings at home, where they sang sentimental songs, played the piano or recited poetry – the works of Tennyson were particularly popular. Others enjoyed trips to see serious operas by artists such as the Italian Giuseppe Verdi (1813-1901), for example at London's impressive Covent Garden opera house. From the 1870s, lighter operettas by Arthur Sullivan and his librettist W.S. Gilbert enjoyed a great vogue (see box page 78).

Melodrama had a wide appeal, and the more lurid examples were very popular with a large lower-class audience. However, by the later Victorian years this audience was largely catered for by the music halls (see box), while plays that attracted a more specifically middle-class audience started to be produced in the 1860s. *Lady Audley's Secret* (1863), adapted by Colin Hazlewood from the 'sensation' novel by Mary Elizabeth Braddon was a melodrama, but its society setting appealed to a middle-class audience.

Social drama

Another development was a type of play that dealt with serious social issues in a realistic way. One of the most important of this type – and one which did not drop out of the repertoire for many years into the 20th century – was *Caste* (1867), by T.W. Robertson (1829-71). Other examples of Robertson's favourite one-word titles show the same serious intent: *Society*, *Progress*, and *War*. *Caste* deals with the issue of class that also preoccupied many novelists, and might even be said to take the concerns of the 'social problem novel' (see box page 23) into drama.

The novelist Charles Reade also showed a serious concern with social issues in his plays. In fact, some of the adaptations he made from his own novels may have taken themselves a little too seriously: a version for the stage of his novel *Put Yourself In His Place* was unsuccessful, possibly partly because it lasted for four and a half hours. Social drama could be successful and profitable, however. *Drink* (1879), a sensational version of Emile Zola's *L'Assommoir*, made Reade £20,000, about five times the earnings of his most successful novel. Another dramatist, Arthur Wing Pinero (1854-1934), made £30,000 from his play about a woman with a past, *The Second Mrs Tanqueray* (1893). With his fashionable upper- and upper middle-class settings, Pinero was a writer of 'society drama' together with the less socially critical Henry Arthur Jones (*The Liars*, 1897) and Oscar Wilde (*Lady Windermere's Fan*, 1892).

Comedy

Comedy took many forms in this period. Pantomimes developed their status as Christmas entertainments before the end of the century.

——— THE MUSIC HALL ———

By the end of the century, the popular theatre was dominated by the music hall, where large audiences were entertained by a varied programme of popular and classical music, comedy, magic, dance and drama. Music hall developed from taverns and drinking halls, and originally the entertainment provided an accompaniment to eating and drinking, with a chairman to introduce the acts (using a 'gavel' like an auctioneer), to keep good order, and to provide a humorous running commentary. The first purpose-built music hall was Morton's Canterbury Hall in London (1852); by the end of the century music halls were everywhere, and the entertainment, rather than the food and drink, became the main reason for going to them.

The motion picture, however, had already gained a toehold in British culture by the end of Victoria's reign, and grew steadily in popularity thereafter. Films were to prove too much for the music halls, which were almost all gone by the end of World War II. But one Victorian carried the tradition of British popular entertainment directly to the movies: Charlie Chaplin, born in London in 1889.

———————

Burlesques, extravaganzas and other similar forms parodied or imitated 'serious' forms of drama such as tragedy. Farce was essentially comedy based on absurd situations, very tight plotting and mistaken identity in which character was completely secondary to plot. The most typical examples were French, in the work of Eugène Labiche and Georges Feydeau. British versions, such as Brandon Thomas's *Charley's Aunt* (1892), were rather less ruthless in their humour than Feydeau's, while recognisably of the same type. Farces were normally in one or two acts. Less common were three-act comedies, which often drew elements from other comic forms or from melodrama. One example, however, is very well-known indeed: Oscar Wilde's *The Importance of Being Earnest* (1895).

Oscar Wilde

Wilde wrote four society comedies – *Lady Windermere's Fan*, *A Woman of No Importance* (1893), *An Ideal Husband* (1895), and *The Importance of Being Earnest* – as well as a one-act tragedy *Salome* (1891). This latter work was composed in French in the hope of a performance at the main Paris theatre, the Comédie-Française. Then Sarah Bernhardt, one of the greatest actresses of the time, agreed to play in it in London, but the Lord Chamberlain's office banned the play (see box page 80). Wilde saw this as a 'triumph for the Philistine', borrowing Matthew Arnold's term (see box page 50). It was not until after Wilde's death that *Salome* became a success – in the form of an opera by the German composer Richard Strauss (1905).

Wilde's comedies show a gradual refinement in his ability to use the form as a vehicle for his extraordinary wit. The first three are, to a certain extent, as much in the mould of social dramas like Pinero's *Second Mrs Tanqueray* as they are comedies, and some influence from melodrama can be discerned as well. Arthur Ransome, now principally known as a children's writer (*Swallows and Amazons*, 1930), published the first study of Wilde in 1912, with some

—— THE SAVOY OPERAS ——

The light operas written by W.S. Gilbert (1836-1911) with Arthur Sullivan (1842-1900) are usually known as the 'Savoy' operas after the theatre that was built for their performance in London by the impresario Richard D'Oyly Carte. Between 1875 (Trial by Jury) *and 1889* (The Gondoliers), *the 'Gilbert and Sullivan' partnership enjoyed success after success. There are frequent elements of parody in both words and music (Gilbert was very familiar with the burlesque mode, and Sullivan, an extremely able composer, easily wrote music in the style of Verdi or Wagner). Gilbert also used biting satire, targeting, for example, the law* in Trial by Jury *and Parliament in* Iolanthe.

A typical example of Gilbert and Sullivan's work is Patience *(1881), which takes as its target the growing Aesthetic Movement (see page 58). The 'fleshly poet' Bunthorne, one of the central characters in the opera, was partly based on Oscar Wilde, and his poem 'Oh, Hollow! Hollow! Hollow!' is a humorous parody of the type of poetry written by Swinburne, Wilde and others. Bunthorne introduces it as 'the wail of the poet's heart on discovering that everything is commonplace. To understand it, cling passionately to one another and think of faint lilies':*

> *What time the poet hath hymned*
> *The writhing maid, lithe-limbed,*
> *   Quivering on amaranthine asphodel,*
> *How can he paint her woes,*
> *Knowing, as he well knows,*
> *   That all can be set right with calomel?*

———————

John Everett Millais, *Ophelia* (1852)

Shakespeare was the inspiration for much in the Victorian period, and this is the most famous tribute by a Victorian to the playwright. Elizabeth Siddal, the model for Ophelia, had to lie in a bathtub for hours while Millais painted the picture.

thoughtful comments on his dramatic work. Ransome felt that Wilde cared little for the plots of his first three plays: 'He consoled himself for his plots by taking extraordinary liberties with them, and amused himself with quips, bon-mots, epigrams and repartee that had really nothing to do with the business in hand.' Ransome considered *The Importance of Being Earnest* a better play mainly because it was honest about its real intent – to explore a fundamentally linguistic world of wit. Its 'very foundation was a pun'. *The Importance of Being Earnest* is full of word-play; for example, Wilde fully exploits the humour in Jack Worthing's having been found as a baby at Victoria Station. As a result, the intensely snobbish Lady Bracknell has concerns about Worthing's ward, Cecily Cardew:

> **Lady Bracknell:** I think some preliminary enquiry on my part would not be out of place. Mr Worthing, is Miss Cardew at all connected with any of the larger railway stations in London? I merely desire information. Until yesterday I had no idea that there were any families or persons whose origin was a Terminus.

—— **THE CENSORS** ——

From 1737 to 1968, all plays for public exhibition in the United Kingdom had to be passed by the Lord Chamberlain's office. Very few plays were in fact banned outright, but, as with all systems of censorship, authors effectively censored themselves in order to have their plays performed. The comparative stability of the British government in the 19th century meant that the Lord Chamberlain's office was somewhat less sensitive about potential political messages in plays than similar authorities in Continental Europe (the setting of Verdi's opera Un ballo in maschera *(1859), for example, had to undergo a bizarre move from Sweden to pre-Revolutionary America to avoid upsetting the censors in Rome). By the end of the century, however, two major dramatists had fallen foul of the Lord Chamberlain's office, albeit on moral rather than political grounds; Wilde's* Salome *and Shaw's play about prostitution,* Mrs Warren's Profession *(1893) both failed to reach the stage.*

Critical responses to Wilde's plays tend to concentrate on three approaches. The first is like Ransome's: that the real interest of the plays is in the verbal pyrotechnics themselves. This would certainly accord well with Wilde's own ideas of pure aesthetics, claiming boldly that 'all art is quite useless'. Another view suggests that beneath the surface wit there is in fact a real basis of sharp social comment and criticism. A third approach is psychological, seeing the double life of, say, Jack Worthing as mirroring the double life Wilde himself had been forced to lead as a homosexual (see Biographical Glossary). There is undoubtedly some truth in all three; it is up to the spectator and the director as to which one becomes prominent in preference to the others.

George Bernard Shaw

Like Wilde, George Bernard Shaw came from the Irish middle class (see Biographical Glossary). He was born in 1856, but wrote many of his plays in the 20th century. He was already an unsuccessful novelist and a successful critic by the time his first play was performed. *Widowers' Houses* (1892) shows the influence of Shaw's left-wing beliefs – in 1884 he was a founder member of the Fabian Society, whose aim was to promote a gradual growth of socialism. The play exposes the injustice of landlords who make huge sums of money from renting out slum properties, and in exposing the hypocrisies and the darker side of middle-class life is strongly reminiscent of the Norwegian dramatist Henrik Ibsen. Ibsen's plays, such as *A Doll's House* (1879) and *An Enemy of the People* (1882), were influential all over Europe and showed a way out of the stale dramatic practices of the 19th century. The social comment in the plays of Reade and Robertson seems tame when compared to the daring treatment of a wife leaving her husband and children (Nora in *A Doll's House*) or of venereal disease (*Ghosts*, 1881). Ibsen also challenged the dramatic conventions of the time; the absence of a 'happy ending' in *A Doll's House* must have appeared very radical.

Shaw was as keen as any to do battle with 19th-century drama, feeling that it lacked substance. He published *The Quintessence of Ibsenism* in 1891 as the first productions of Ibsen were being shown in London. It was therefore ironic that some of Shaw's earlier work was nevertheless influenced by theatrical practices that he might have been expected to avoid at all costs; there is more than a hint of the *pièce bien faite* about the ending of *Widowers' Houses*, for example, and *The Devil's Disciple* (1897) is openly melodramatic. Yet even in this play there is a seriousness of theme and social comment that is absent from a work such as *Black-Ey'd Susan*, and certainly absent from the more downmarket melodramas in the popular theatres. In fact, bringing serious issues to bear on the London stage was the main achievement of Shaw's work in the 1890s, for example the debunking of romantic ideas of war in *Arms and the Man* (1894); and the examination of middle-class *attitudes* to prostitution, in *Mrs Warren's Profession* (1893, not performed until 1902 – see box page 80).

ACTORS

The 19th century saw the rise of a system based on star performers; audiences went to see the star as often as they did the play. The leading man and the leading lady were the key actors in any company, able to play the major Shakespearean roles. There were also other actors who specialised in particular types of role, such as a villain in melodrama or the 'juvenile lead', who would play the young lover. The range of types varied, but the company tended to have plays written for it which suited the character types on offer. This, coupled with the idea of the 'well-made play', meant that Victorian plays often showed little overall variety. Well-known stars included Charles Kean (1811-68), the American Edward Booth (1833-93), and Henry Irving (1838-1905). Irving and Ellen Terry (1847-1928) were the leading lights of the late Victorian theatrical scene. Bram Stoker, the author of Dracula, *spent much of his life as Irving's agent, and wrote a memoir of him when he died. Irving and Terry's interpretations of Shakespeare were particularly admired.*

TIMELINE

Science, technology and the arts	Literature	History
	1829 Jerrold *Black-Ey'd Susan*	**1829** Catholic emancipation
1830-3 Lyell *Principles of Geology*		**1830** Opening of Liverpool and Manchester Railway
1831-6 Voyage of HMS *Beagle*		**1831** Population of United Kingdom 24 million
		1832 First Reform Act
from 1833 Newman and others *Tracts for the Times*	**1833** Death of Arthur Hallam; Tennyson begins poems inspired by him	**1833** Slavery abolished in British Empire
	1834 Lytton *The Last Days of Pompeii*	**1834** Poor Law Amendment Act
1835 Fox Talbot develops photographic technology	**1835-6** Gautier *Mademoiselle de Maupin*	
1836 Pugin *Contrasts*	**1836-7** Dickens *Sketches by Boz*, *The Pickwick Papers*	
1837 Isaac Pitman develops a system of shorthand	**1838** Dickens *Oliver Twist*	**1837** Victoria comes to the throne
1838 Launch of Brunel's *Great Western*	**1838-9** Dickens *Nicholas Nickleby*	**1838** People's Charter
1839-55 Michael Faraday *Researches in Electricity*		
	1840-1 Dickens *The Old Curiosity Shop*	**1840** Victoria marries Prince Albert; Introduction of the Penny Post
1842 Richard Owen invents the word 'dinosaur'; Comte *Course in Positive Philosophy* (started 1830)		**1842** Chadwick reports on the sanitary conditions of the working class
1843 Ruskin *Modern Painters*; Launch of Brunel's *Great Britain*		
1844 Carlyle *Past and Present*	**1844** Disraeli *Coningsby*	
	1845 Marriage of Robert and Elizabeth Browning; Disraeli *Sybil*	**1845-6** Height of the Irish Famine
1846 Strauss *The Life of Jesus* (translated into English by George Eliot)	**1845-6** Dickens *Dombey and Son*	**1846** Repeal of the Corn Laws
	1847 Charlotte Brontë *Jane Eyre*; Emily Brontë *Wuthering Heights*; Anne Brontë *Agnes Grey*; Thackeray *Vanity Fair* (to 1848)	
1848 Marx and Engels *The Communist Manifesto*; Foundation of the Pre-Raphaelite Brotherhood	**1848** Gaskell *Mary Barton*; Trollope *The Kellys and the O'Kellys*; Dickens *Dombey and Son*	**1848** 'Year of Revolutions' in continental Europe; Last Chartist petition; Public Health Act
1849 Millais's painting *Lorenzo and Isabella*; Ruskin *The Seven Lamps of Architecture*		**1849** Disraeli becomes Conservative leader

1851 Ruskin *Pre-Raphaelitism*, *The Stones of Venice* (to 1853)
1852 Canterbury Hall (first music hall) opens in London; Completion of Barry and Pugin's neo-Gothic Houses of Parliament in London
1854 Hunt's painting *The Awakening Conscience*; John Snow identifies contaminated water as the cause of a cholera and typhoid epidemic in London

1856 First London performance of Verdi's opera *La Traviata*
1858 Launch of Brunel's *Great Eastern*

1859 Darwin *On the Origin of Species*; Smiles *Self-Help*

1861 Development of the germ theory of disease by Louis Pasteur; Foundation of the Royal Academy of Music
1862 Frith's painting *The Railway Station*
1863 Ford Madox Brown's painting *Work*; J.S. Mill *Utilitarianism*

1865 Outcry in Paris at nudity in Manet's painting *Déjeuner sur l'herbe*

1849-50 Dickens *David Copperfield*
1850 Elizabeth Browning *Sonnets from the Portuguese*; Wordsworth *The Prelude* (revised version); Tennyson *In Memoriam*; Tennyson becomes Poet Laureate on Wordsworth's death
1851-3 Gaskell *Cranford*

1852-3 Dickens *Bleak House*
1853 Arnold *Poems*

1854 Dickens *Hard Times*
1855 Robert Browning *Men and Women*; Trollope *The Warden*; Tennyson *Maud*; Gaskell *North and South*; Dickens *Little Dorrit* (to 1857)
1856 Elizabeth Browning *Aurora Leigh*
1857 Hughes *Tom Brown's School Days*; Gaskell *The Life of Charlotte Brontë*; Baudelaire *Les Fleurs du Mal*
1859 Eliot *Adam Bede*

1860 Boucicault *The Colleen Bawn*; Eliot *The Mill on the Floss*; Dickens *Great Expectations* (to 1861)

1862 Clough *Amours de Voyage*; Christina Rossetti *Goblin Market and Other Poems*; Braddon *Lady Audley's Secret*
1864-5 Dickens *Our Mutual Friend*
1865 Swinburne *Atalanta in Calydon*

1851 Great Exhibition

1853-6 Crimean War

1855 Abolition of stamp duty on newspapers

1857 Indian Mutiny
1858 India brought under direct British control

1861 Death of Prince Albert; Abolition of paper duty; Beginning of the American Civil War (to 1865)

1863 Foundation of Football Association

Science, technology and the arts	Literature	History
1866 Completion of Birch's West Pier at Brighton	**1866** Eliot *Felix Holt, the Radical*; Gaskell *Wives and Daughters*	**1866** Livingstone goes missing on his final exploration in Africa
1867 Johann Strauss II's *Blue Danube* waltz first heard in Vienna	**1867** Robertson *Caste*	**1867** Second Reform Act; Canada given Dominion status
	1868 Collins *The Moonstone*	**1868** Both Disraeli and Gladstone become Prime Minister for the first time
	1869 Matthew Arnold *Culture and Anarchy*	
	1870 Dickens *Edwin Drood*	**1870** Forster's Education Act; Franco-Prussian War (to 1871)
1871 Darwin *The Descent of Man*	**1871-2** Eliot *Middlemarch*	**1871** Population of United Kingdom 31.5 million; Trade Union Act
1872 Completion of Gilbert Scott's Albert Memorial in London		**1872** Introduction of the secret ballot; Founding of National Agricultural Labourers' Union
1873 Pater *Studies in the History of the Renaissance*		**1873** Foundation of the Home Rule League in Ireland
1875 Whistler's painting *Old Battersea Bridge*; Gilbert and Sullivan's comic opera *Trial by Jury* opens in London	**1874** Hardy *Far from the Madding Crowd*	
1876 Completion of Wagner's *Ring* cycle of four operas	**1876** Eliot *Daniel Deronda*	**1876** Queen Victoria becomes Empress of India
1877 Monet's painting *Gare St-Lazare*		
1878 Joseph Swan produces the first practical light bulb	**1878** Hardy *The Return of the Native*	
1879 Dante Gabriel Rossetti's painting *The Blessèd Damozel*	**1879** Ibsen *A Doll's House*; foundation of the *Boys' Own Paper*	
		1880 Parnell elected Chairman of the Home Rule Party
1881 Gilbert and Sullivan's comic opera *Patience*; Completion of Waterhouse's Natural History Museum building in London	**1881** Rossetti *The House of Life*; Christina Rossetti *Monna Innominata*	
1882 Completion of Street's Law Courts in the Strand, London		**1882** Irish Chief Secretary is murdered in Dublin
1883 Foundation of the Royal College of Music	**1883** Trollope *Autobiography*	**1884** Foundation of Fabian Society
1884 Seurat's painting *Bathers at Asnières*		**from mid-1880s** 'Scramble for Africa' begins

*c.*1885 Completion of Norman Shaw's Cragside, Northumberland

1887 Stanford, Irish Symphony; Verdi's opera *Otello*, based on Shakespeare's play; Cézanne's picture of *Mont Ste-Victoire with Large Pine Trees*

1891 Morris founds the Kelmscott Press

1893 Munch's painting *The Scream*
1894 Debussy's *Prélude à l'après-midi d'un faune*

1896 Marconi patents wireless telegraphy

1897 Ronald Ross discovers that malaria is transmitted by mosquitoes; Vaccine against typhoid
1898 The Curies discover radium and polonium
1899 First of Monet's *Water Lily* pictures; Rennie Mackintosh completes the Glasgow School of Art building
1900 Elgar's oratorio *The Dream of Gerontius*; Puccini's opera *Tosca*

1885 Haggard *King Solomon's Mines*

1886 Stevenson *The Strange Case of Dr Jekyll and Mr Hyde*; Hardy *The Mayor of Casterbridge*
1887 Doyle *A Study in Scarlet*; Haggard *She*
1888 Isabella Ward *Robert Elsmere*

1890 Morris *News from Nowhere*; Wilde *The Picture of Dorian Grey*
1891 Gissing *New Grub Street*; Hardy *Tess of the d'Urbervilles*; Wilde *Salome*
1892 George and Weedon Grossmith *The Diary of a Nobody*; Shaw *Widowers' Houses*; Wilde *Lady Windermere's Fan*
1893 Pinero *The Second Mrs Tanqueray*; Wilde *A Woman of No Importance*
1894 Collapse of the three-volume novel system; Shaw *Arms and the Man*
1895 Hardy *Jude the Obscure*; Wells *The Time Machine*; Wilde *The Importance of Being Earnest*
1897 Hardy *Wessex Poems*; Stoker *Dracula*

1885 General Gordon dies at Khartoum

1886 Failure of Home Rule Bill; Split in Liberal Party

1887 Victoria's Golden Jubilee
1888 'Jack the Ripper' murders in Whitechapel, London
1890 Fall of Parnell over his involvement in a divorce case

1893 Foundation of Independent Labour Party
1893-4 Second Home Rule Bill fails; Resignation of Gladstone

1897 Victoria's Diamond Jubilee

1899-1902 Boer War

1900 Australia given Dominion status
1901 Death of Queen Victoria; Population of United Kingdom 41.5 million

8 5

GLOSSARY OF TERMS

Act of Union The Act of Union of 1800 joined England in a legislative union with Ireland. A similar Act in 1707 had joined England and Scotland. The United Kingdom of Great Britain and Ireland formed by these two acts was ruled from Westminster. See also *Unionist*.

Aestheticism This movement, inspired by French authors such as Théophile Gautier (1811-72) and Charles Baudelaire (1821-67), arose in the British arts in the 1880s and advocated an art based on pure beauty and the pleasures of the senses ('art for art's sake') rather than on morality or on social comment.

agnostic An agnostic believes that God's existence cannot be certainly known (which would be the position of a theist) or certainly denied (by an atheist). Many Victorian thinkers were agnostics.

Anglican A member of the Church of England, the state or 'established' church in England (not the rest of the United Kingdom). Set up by Henry VIII in the 16th century, it combines Protestant and Catholic features (though it is not part of the Roman Catholic Church) and as a result some of its members emphasise different aspects of its traditions (see *Anglo-Catholic*, *High Church* and *Evangelical*).

Anglo-Catholic An *Anglican* who emphasises the Catholic aspects of the Church of England, with services based on ritual similar to that used by traditional Roman Catholics.

Anti-Corn Law League Formed by businessmen in Manchester in 1838 because they wanted to repeal the Corn Laws of 1815 (with other amendments) which made importing foreign corn prohibitively expensive. The Prime Minister Robert Peel finally managed to push through the repeal of the Corn Laws in 1846.

Arts and Crafts Movement An artistic movement (particularly in architecture and the applied arts) of the later 19th century, which emphasised traditional hand-crafted products as a reaction against mechanised, industrial production. William Morris was a leading figure.

Ascendancy The term used for the Protestant middle and upper class of landowners in Ireland (the majority of their tenants being Roman Catholic). Many were 'absentees' who lived in England, though some were active in Ireland.

Bentham(ite) Jeremy Bentham (1748-1832) was a *Utilitarian* thinker who believed that actions are right if they achieve 'the happiness of the greatest number'. Opponents of the Benthamite philosophy usually concentrated on the fate of the minority interests who did not form part of 'the greatest number' and were thus marginalised.

blank verse The standard metre of Shakespeare's plays and of much later verse, including much from the Victorian period. There are five stresses in each line and the lines do not rhyme.

burlesque A style that mocks particular types of writing by imitating them. Very like a parody, which tends to be used when one specific work or author is imitated. Both are usually humorous.

Chartism A mainly working-class *radical* movement of the late 1830s and 1840s whose demands for governmental reform were outlined in the 'People's Charter' (see page 10).

Classical (or Neo-classical) In the arts, 'classical' works are those based on the harmony, logic and strong sense of proportion found in Greek and Roman art. Classical thinking tends to emphasise reason rather than emotion. Typical of literature and art in the mid-18th century, after which *Romantic* styles took over, but classical styles were still common in 19th-century architecture (Newcastle city centre is the most extensive example).

Conservative Conservatism emphasises the values of tradition and keeping to established ways of doing things. It is associated with the Right in politics. In the mid-19th century the Tory party developed into the Conservative party; its best-known leader was Benjamin Disraeli.

Decadent Movement A loose term for a fashionable late 19th-century artistic movement which emphasised atmosphere, sensual experience and, especially, the dark side of the human psyche.

didactic A term describing a work which aims to teach its audience a lesson, often a moral one.

dramatic monologue A Victorian form of poem, sometimes in *blank verse*, in which a character reveals him- or herself to the reader in an extended solo speech. Tennyson and Browning are the best-known writers in this style.

Eclecticism A style of artistic expression which draws on many different influences and sources.

emancipation The term means 'freeing'; in 1829 it referred to the Act which granted Roman Catholics the right to sit in Parliament and hold other state offices.

epic A long verse narrative on a specific central theme, often with a hero figure at the centre. Homer (in Greek) and Virgil (in Latin) are the usual models. The term can also be used of any work which shows 'epic' qualities.

Evangelical A member of the Anglican Church who emphasises its Protestant features; services are simple, without ritual and based strongly on the words of the Bible. There is also a strong emphasis on converting others to the faith.

evolution A process of gradual change; the word is used to refer to the process by which biological species slowly change and acquire different characteristics, suggested by Darwin and others.

genre A type of writing: the main literary genres of poetry, prose and drama can be sub-divided into genres of novel, short story, epic, comedy, tragedy and so on.

Gothic The style of art and architecture based, in particular, on the pointed arch, typical of the European Middle Ages. In the 19th century there was a revival of interest in this style, particularly in north-western Europe (including Britain) and North America.

High Church An *Anglican* who emphasises the Catholic tradition of the Church of England; very like an Anglo-Catholic but not necessarily quite as extreme.

Home Rule The late 19th-century movement demanding some form of self-rule in Ireland.

Industrial Revolution A general term for the process by which the economy in Britain, Belgium, France, Germany, the United States and other countries moved away from an exclusively agricultural base to one which emphasised mechanised production of manufactured goods, iron and steel.

Liberal Liberalism traditionally emphasises freedom of beliefs, of trade and of the individual. The Liberal party emerged in Britain during the mid-19th century and appealed to the skilled working class and to the new middle classes.

medievalism An interest in and attempt to reproduce the artistic styles and themes of the Middle Ages. Medievalism was an important influence in the Victorian period.

melodrama A type of play with simple characters and straightforward plots which relied heavily on playing on the emotions of the audience. Sentiment, fear and shock were especially prominent. The word 'melodramatic' can also be used when a similar style is used in a novel or a poem.

natural selection In the theory of *evolution*, the way in which characteristics best adapted for survival in the natural world will be 'selected' and preserved, while other characteristics – and species – will die out.

Nonconformist A member of a Protestant church who is not an Anglican. There are large numbers of different sects, some more radical than others: Methodists, Baptists, Congregationalists, Presbyterians, Plymouth Brethren and Quakers are some of the more commonly encountered groups.

Oxford Movement A *High Church* movement of the 1830s and after that originated in tracts written by Cardinal Newman and others (see page 63), which aimed to revive traditional Catholic beliefs and ceremony.

Peelite After the repeal of the Corn Laws in 1846 there was a split in the Conservative party between those who had supported Robert Peel and those who opposed him. Peel's supporters were called 'Peelites' and effectively formed a different political group from the Conservative party. Lord Aberdeen was a Peelite Prime Minister from 1852 to 1855.

Philistinism This term comes from Matthew Arnold's essay *Culture and Anarchy* (see page 50). He divided society into three sections: upper-class 'Barbarians', the working-class 'Populace', and the middle-class 'Philistines'. This last group were the strongest and the most influential, but lacked what he called the 'sweetness and light' of Culture, the 'study of perfection' whose aim is to 'render an intelligent being more intelligent'. A 'Philistine' has thus come to mean a person with an interest in material possessions, but no real interest in culture.

Positivism Positivist thought, which was very prominent in European philosophy in the 19th century (largely under the influence of Auguste Comte, see page 69) suggests that all genuine knowledge is the result of scientific research. Any knowledge which is 'metaphysical' – that is, derived from speculation or intuition of something from 'beyond' the material, physical world, including traditional religious belief – is therefore to be rejected as unreliable.

Pre-Raphaelite Brotherhood (PRB) An artistic group formed by William Holman Hunt, Dante Gabriel Rossetti, Sir John Everett Millais and four others in 1848. They took their inspiration from 15th-century styles of painting before Raphael. Many of the members also took a close interest in literature.

Radical Radicals argue for more extensive political or social change than that put forward by mainstream political groups. They tend to be on the left of the political spectrum and are often regarded with mistrust by members of the established middle and upper classes. *Chartism* was a radical movement.

Ragged Schools These were charitable institutions set up to provide education and training for poor children. They died out quickly after the Education Act of 1870 provided compulsory state elementary education.

Romantic movement The Romantics emphasised the life of the emotions rather than that of reason (as seen in *Classical* or *Neo-classical* art). The movement grew up in the later 18th century and was particularly strong in English literature from about 1790 to 1830. Authors include William Wordsworth, Samuel Taylor Coleridge and Lord Byron. 'Romantic' works typically emphasise the life of the individual.

social problem novel (also the 'Condition of England' novel and the 'industrial novel')

A novel concerned with the special difficulties of Victorian times, for example conditions in factories.

Stoic(ism) Stoicism was a Greek and Roman philosophical movement which suggested that all people were governed by the same natural laws, so the best course of action was to accept what happened with a good grace as being inevitable. It influenced many with a strong classical education, like Matthew Arnold.

three-decker A novel published in three volumes. This method of publishing novels was popular throughout the Victorian period, but came to an end in 1894.

tract An essay arguing a case on a religious subject; specifically used by the originators of the *Oxford Movement* to describe the pamphlets and longer publications in which they expressed their views.

Tractarian An alternative name for a member of the Oxford Movement.

Unionist A supporter of the Union of Great Britain and Ireland (now a supporter of the union of Great Britain and Northern Ireland). It was a division between Unionists and supporters of *Home Rule* that split the Liberal Party in 1886.

Unitarianism A religious group which denied the divinity of Christ and insisted on the unity of God – that is, a God not 'divided' into Father, Son and Holy Spirit. Popular with the Victorian middle classes, its most famous member was the novelist Elizabeth Gaskell.

Utilitarianism A major movement in 19th-century philosophy which judged an act as morally right or wrong according to how many people's happiness was affected by it (see *Bentham*, its founder). In the mid-century it affected economic thought profoundly; there was a considerable emphasis on the idea that the market would regulate itself to produce happiness for the greatest number. Its critics pointed in particular to its tendency to ignore the needs of the weak and of minorities and to its strictly logical approach, which could seem ruthless and lacking in sympathy.

BIOGRAPHICAL GLOSSARY

Arnold, Matthew (1822-88) poet and critic. Son of Dr Thomas Arnold, headmaster of Rugby School and educational reformer. Matthew Arnold was educated at Rugby and at Oxford University, where he became professor of poetry (1857-67). From 1851, he was an inspector of schools. Many of his poems express the doubts and uncertainties of the Victorian age, the most famous being 'Dover Beach'. He also wrote many works of literary and social criticism.

Brontë, Charlotte (1816-55); **Emily** (1818-48); **Anne** (1820-49) novelists. Three of the six children born to an Ulster-born clergyman, Patrick Brontë, and his Cornish wife Maria. In 1820 the family moved to Haworth, a village on the edge of the moors near Keighley in Yorkshire. Maria Brontë died a year later. The four eldest Brontë girls, Maria, Elizabeth, Charlotte and Emily were sent away to boarding school in 1824, but after the deaths of the two eldest girls from consumption, Charlotte and Emily returned home. After this time the Brontës were educated at home, reading widely and creating their own elaborate fantasy worlds. Charlotte and her brother, Branwell, wrote stories about the kingdom of Angria, while Emily and Anne created the Gondal saga. In adulthood, all three sisters became governesses, with varying degrees of success. In the early 1840s, Charlotte planned to set up a school at home, and in order to gain more experience she and Emily went to teach in Brussels. Then, in 1845, Charlotte discovered some poems written by Emily, and the following year a selection of poems written by the three sisters was published under the pseudonyms Currer, Ellis and Acton Bell. All three had also completed novels: *Jane Eyre* (by Charlotte), *Wuthering Heights* (by Emily) and *Agnes Grey* (by Anne) were published in 1847. Anne's *The Tenant of Wildfell Hall* appeared in 1848. In that same year, Charlotte and Anne visited London in order to quell the various rumours about the identities of Currer, Ellis and Acton Bell. Emily died in December 1848, and Anne the following year, both of tuberculosis. Charlotte went on to publish *Shirley* (1849) and *Villette* (1853). She married in 1854, but died the following year from complications during pregnancy.

Browning, Elizabeth Barrett (1806-61) poet. Born at Coxhoe Hall, Durham, her family moved to Herefordshire three years later. She was educated at home, and began to write at an early age. In 1820, Elizabeth's father, Edward Moulton Barrett arranged for the private publication of an epic written by his eldest daughter, *The Battle of Marathon*. From 1821 until 1846, Elizabeth was an invalid, confined to her room and suffering numerous illnesses. Her condition was exacerbated by the death by drowning of her brother in 1838. Throughout this time she wrote poetry, publishing several volumes, including *Poems* (1844). The poet Robert Browning so admired her verse that he wrote to her, and the two began a correspondence, meeting in 1845 and marrying secretly in 1846, as their liaison was violently opposed by Elizabeth's father. Robert and Elizabeth moved to Italy, settling in Florence where they became part of a famous literary circle. Their son, Robert, was born in 1849. Elizabeth continued to publish poetry, including *Sonnets from the Portuguese* (1850) recording her love for her husband ('Portuguese' was his pet name for her, because of her dark complexion). She died in her husband's arms in Florence in 1861.

Browning, Robert (1812-89) poet. Born in London, educated at home where his father, a clerk in the Bank of England, had an extensive library. He studied briefly at the University of London before leaving in his second term. His first published poem was 'Pauline' (1833), which attracted little notice, but 'Paracelsus' (1835) was more successful. Browning travelled to Russia and Italy, and from 1841-6 his work was published in a series of pamphlets called *Bells and Pomegranates*. In 1845 Browning began to correspond with Elizabeth Barrett whose *Poems* he had greatly admired. They married secretly in 1846 and settled in Florence, where they remained until Elizabeth's death in 1861. Their son, Robert, was born in 1849. Browning's popularity grew with the publication of *Men and Women* (1855), *Dramatis Personae* (1864) and *The Ring and the Book* (1868-9). After Elizabeth's death, he returned to live in London. His reputation was confirmed by the formation of the Browning Society in 1881. He died in Venice in 1889.

Carlyle, Thomas (1795-1881) historian, essayist and critic. Born in Ecclefechan, Scotland, his parents intended him to become a minister in the Presbyterian Church, but after attending Edinburgh University and studying briefly for the ministry, he abandoned this idea. He taught for a while before starting a career in literary work, writing and reviewing. In 1821, he married Jane Welsh, herself a considerable scholar. Carlyle wrote many works in his long career including *Sartor Resartus* (1833-4), *History of the French Revolution* (1837) and *Past and Present* (1843). He was an extremely influential figure in Victorian society, and no one in the literary circles of the period remained untouched by his writing and opinions, notably his celebration of the individual. Jane Carlyle died in 1866, Carlyle in 1881. He was buried, according to his wishes, in his birthplace, Ecclefechan.

Clough, Arthur Hugh (1819-61) poet. Son of a Liverpool cotton merchant, he went to Rugby School, where he met and became a friend of Matthew Arnold, and then to Oxford University. At Oxford his religious beliefs were challenged, and he was tormented by doubt. He wrote two verse novels, *The Bothie of Tober-na-Vuolich* (1848) and *Amours de Voyage* (1862) as well as shorter poems. He died aged only 42 in Venice. Matthew Arnold's elegy, 'Thyrsis', is in memory of him.

Collins, Wilkie (1824-89) novelist. Son of the landscape painter, William Collins. He was educated at private schools, and was set to become a lawyer. But the publication of his first book, a biography of his father, signalled a change of career. He met Dickens in 1851 and wrote many articles for *Household Words* and *All the Year Round*, becoming a close friend of the Dickens family. Collins was best known for his 'sensational' novels, particularly *The Woman in White* (1860) and *The Moonstone* (1868). Collins's health declined after 1870, partly as a result of his addiction to laudanum. Nevertheless he continued to write novels which were well-received by the general public.

Darwin, Charles (1809-82) natural historian. Born in Shrewsbury and educated at Cambridge and Edinburgh universities. Although a medical student at Edinburgh, he became interested in geology and was recommended for the post of naturalist on board HMS *Beagle*, a survey ship bound for South America. During the voyage of the *Beagle*, from 1831 to 1836, Darwin observed all aspects of the environments he visited, and on his return he published a *Journal* of his travels. He went on to formulate the theory of natural selection (see Glossary of Terms), but delayed publication because of the controversy he knew it would excite. *On the Origin of Species by means of Natural Selection* was published in 1859. *The Descent of Man* appeared in 1871 and made clear the place of humans in Darwin's theory of evolution.

Dickens, Charles (1812-70) novelist. Born in Portsmouth, Dickens spent much of his early life in Chatham, Kent before his family moved to London. His father got into debt and in 1824 was imprisoned in the Marshalsea Debtors' Prison for a time. At the same time Dickens was sent to work in a shoe-blacking factory, an experience which was to mark him for the remainder of his life. Dickens went on to become a lawyer's clerk, and then a journalist, often using the pseudonym 'Boz'. *Sketches by Boz* (1836-7) and *The Pickwick Papers* (1837) launched his meteoric rise to fame. In 1836 Dickens married Catherine Hogarth and they went on to have ten children. All the time

Dickens continued to write at a hectic pace, as well as editing a weekly periodical *Household Words* (*All the Year Round* after 1859) and participating in amateur dramatics. Most of Dickens's novels were published in serial form and probably reached a larger audience than the works of any other major Victorian novelist. Dickens toured North America in 1842 and made extended visits to Italy and Switzerland later in the 1840s. In 1857, he met an actress called Ellen Ternan and a year later he separated from his wife. From 1858 onwards, Dickens undertook a series of public readings from his works. These reading tours were hugely successful, taking him once again to North America in 1867-8. However, his health suffered; in June 1870 he collapsed and died at his home, Gadshill near Rochester. He was buried with full honours in Westminster Abbey.

Disraeli, Benjamin (1804-81) politician and novelist. Son of the writer Isaac d'Israeli, Benjamin was educated at private schools and in his father's extensive library. He went to Lincoln's Inn Fields to study law but gave it up, going on to establish a daily newspaper *The Representative* which failed after a few months. His first novel *Vivian Grey* (1826) was written partly to try to recoup some money from this loss. Disraeli became involved in politics after 1832, becoming Conservative MP for Maidstone in 1839. His concern for the conditions of the poor is reflected in his novels *Coningsby* (1844) and *Sybil* (1845). He was Prime Minister in 1868, and again 1874-80.

Eliot, George (1819-80) pen-name of the novelist Mary Ann (Marian) Evans. Born in Arbury, Warwickshire. Her father Robert was a land agent; her mother died in 1836 and soon after Mary Ann took over the running of the household. Mary Ann had been sent to boarding school at the age of five, and after her mother's death her father encouraged her obvious intellectual ability by employing tutors to teach her German, Italian and Latin. In 1841, Mary Ann moved with her father to Coventry, where she met Charles Bray and his brother-in-law Charles Hennell, whose influence led her to reject the Evangelical Christianity of her youth. After her father's death in 1849, Mary Ann toured Europe, settling in London on her return. She began to write for the *Westminster Review*, becoming part of a literary circle whose members included the writer George Henry Lewes. She and Lewes lived together from 1854 until his death in 1878. Her first novel *Adam Bede* (1859) was a great success, and was followed by *The Mill on the Floss* (1860), *Silas Marner* (1861), *Romola* (1863), *Felix Holt* (1866) and *Middlemarch* (1871-2). After Lewes's death, Mary Ann married John Walter Cross in 1880. She died a few months later.

Gaskell, Elizabeth (1810-65) novelist. Daughter of a Unitarian minister (see Glossary of Terms), she was brought up by an aunt in Knutsford, Cheshire. In 1832 she married William Gaskell, also a Unitarian minister and settled in Manchester. The Gaskells had four daughters, and a son who died in infancy. *Mary Barton* (1848) was written to distract Elizabeth from the grief of losing him. Dickens admired the novel and invited Mrs Gaskell to contribute to *Household Words* and *All the Year Round*. *Cranford* (1853), *North and South* (1855) and others followed. In 1850 Mrs Gaskell met Charlotte Brontë and after Charlotte's death five years later, she wrote a biography of her friend. Mrs Gaskell herself died suddenly in 1865, leaving her last novel *Wives and Daughters* (1866) unfinished.

Gissing, George (1857-1903) novelist. Educated at a Quaker school in Alderley Edge, Cheshire, he went to college in Manchester but was expelled for stealing and went to prison for a month. He travelled in America before settling in London where he survived by teaching Latin and Greek. He married twice; neither marriage was successful. Secretive and obsessed with his writing, he had few friends apart from the novelist H.G. Wells. Neverthless he was a hardworking and prolific writer, producing over 20 novels, the best-known of which are *New Grub Street* (1891) and *The Odd Women* (1893).

Hardy, Thomas (1840-1928) novelist and poet. Born in Higher Bockhampton, near Dorchester, he was educated locally and in Dorchester. In 1856 he became apprenticed to an architect and in 1862 moved to London to work for Arthur Blomfield. He met his first wife Emma while working on a church restoration at St Juliot in Cornwall and married in 1874. His first published novel was *Desperate Remedies* (1871), and the success of his writing allowed him to give up his career as an architect. He and Emma lived sometimes in London, sometimes in Dorset (Sturminster Newton and Wimborne), but by 1885 they had a permanent home at Max Gate on the edge of Dorchester. After the 1890s Hardy wrote no more fiction, but published *Wessex Poems* in 1897; from 1902 to 1928 he produced eight more major collections of poetry. Emma died in 1912, after a less than ideal marriage in its latter stages, and he remarried in 1914.

Hopkins, Gerard Manley (1844-89) poet. At Highgate School in London he won the poetry prize in 1860; he went on to Oxford University where he came under the influence of Cardinal Newman and the Oxford Movement (see Glossary of Terms). In 1868, he became a Jesuit, becoming ordained as a priest in 1877. Although Hopkins had continued to write poetry at Oxford, he wrote little while training to be a priest. He started again in 1875, when he wrote 'The Wreck of the *Deutschland'*, dedicated to five Franciscan nuns who died when the ship sank in the Thames estuary. Hopkins continued to write in subsequent years, but never tried to publish his work. He died of typhoid in 1889: a collection of his poems was finally published in 1918.

Mill, John Stuart (1806-73) philosopher and economist. Educated by his father, James Mill, who was a colleague of Jeremy Bentham and a firm believer in Utilitarianism (see Glossary of Terms). In 1823 Mill started work for the East India Company, at the same time writing articles for periodicals. Three years later he had a crisis which led him to question Utilitarian doctrines and to embrace the poetry of Wordsworth with its emphasis on emotion. In 1831 he met Harriet Taylor who had a major intellectual influence upon him: they married in 1851. He was an independent MP for Westminster from 1865-8. Mill was an influential liberal writer of the 19th century: some of his best-known works include *The System of Logic* (1843), *Utilitarianism* (1861) and *The Subjection of Women* (1869).

Newman, John Henry (1801-90) theologian and writer. Educated privately, he went to Oxford University and became involved in the Oxford Movement (see Glossary of Terms). In 1841, he published a tract arguing that the 39 Articles of the Anglican Church were compatible with Roman Catholicism. This led to the official banning of Tractarianism. In 1845 Newman became a Roman Catholic, causing a rift with fellow members of the Oxford Movement. His most celebrated work *Apologia pro Vita Sua* (1864) was written in response to criticism by the novelist Charles Kingsley. Newman also wrote *The Dream of Gerontius* (1832), later set to music by Edward Elgar.

Rossetti, Dante Gabriel (1828-82) poet and painter; **Christina** (1830-94) poet. Two children of the Rossetti family, born and educated in London. Dante Gabriel studied painting with Holman Hunt and John Everett Millais, and with them and others formed the Pre-Raphaelite Brotherhood in 1848 (see page 54). In 1850 Rossetti met Elizabeth Siddal, a 'stunner' (a PRB term) whom he eventually married in 1860. She died two years later from an overdose of laudanum, and Rossetti buried the manuscripts of several of his poems with her body (they were later exhumed). Rossetti continued to paint, and to publish poetry and translations of Italian works. He also produced designs for William Morris's firm. In later life he became a recluse, attempting suicide in 1872. His sister, Christina, was also associated with the PRB, becoming engaged to the Pre-Raphaelite painter William Collinson although they did not marry. She was a devoutly committed High Anglican, influenced by the Oxford Movement (see Glossary of Terms). Although an invalid for much of her life, she published many collections of verse including

Goblin Market (1862), and *Time Flies: A reading diary* (1885) a compilation of poems and thoughts for each day.

Ruskin, John (1819-1900) art critic. An only child, he was educated at home and travelled on the Continent with his parents from an early age. When he went to Oxford University in 1836, his mother accompanied him. He became devoted to the paintings of J.M.W. Turner, and championed his cause in *Modern Painters* (1843). With the publication of *The Seven Lamps of Architecture* (1849) and *The Stones of Venice* (1851-3), Ruskin became the foremost art critic in Britain. He also supported the work of the Pre-Raphaelite Brotherhood. In 1848 he married Euphemia (Effie) Chalmers Gray, but the marriage was annulled on the grounds of Ruskin's impotence. Effie went on to marry the painter John Everett Millais. Ruskin continued to write and lecture on art, as well as becoming involved in social and economic issues. In 1870, he became the first Slade Professor of Fine Arts at Oxford. He spent his last years at Brantwood, his house in the Lake District.

Stevenson, Robert Louis (1850-94) novelist, travel writer and children's author. Born in Edinburgh, in childhood and throughout his life he was dogged by ill health. He was nevertheless an enthusiastic traveller, publishing amongst others *Travels with a Donkey* (1879) describing a journey through the Cévennes region of France. In 1879 he went to the USA, marrying there Mrs Fanny Osbourne whom he had met three years earlier in France. He wrote *Treasure Island* (1883) for her son, Lloyd. It was a huge success, and he followed it with *The Strange Case of Dr Jekyll and Mr Hyde* ((1886), *Kidnapped* (1886) and *The Master of Ballantrae* (1889). In 1888, in search of a climate more suitable for his frail health, Stevenson set sail with his family for the Pacific islands. He was never to return to Britain. He died in Samoa in 1894.

Tennyson, Alfred (Lord) 1809-92 poet. Born in Lincolnshire, he was the son of a clergyman and went to Trinity College, Cambridge. His first book *Poems, Chiefly Lyrical* (1830) echoed Wordsworth and Coleridge's *Lyrical Ballads*. In 1833, Arthur Hallam, a friend from university, died suddenly on a trip to Vienna. Hallam was engaged to Tennyson's sister, Emily, and his relationship with Tennyson himself was extremely intense. Various of Tennyson's poems owe their existence to the period of self-questioning and doubt that followed this event. In 1850 he succeeded Wordsworth as Poet Laureate, and married Emily Sellwood to whom he had been engaged for many years. The couple went to live on the Isle of Wight and had a son, Hallam. Tennyson continued to write: *Maud and other Poems* (1855) and *Idylls of the King* (1859) confirmed his fame. He had several audiences with Queen Victoria, and was made a baronet in 1883.

Thackeray, William Makepeace (1811-63) novelist. Born in Calcutta, India, where his father worked for the East India Company. His father died when he was three and he was sent home to England in 1817. He went to Cambridge University where he lost part of his inheritance in gambling debts. He travelled to Paris, and to Germany where he met the poet Goethe. On his return to London he wrote for a newspaper and studied art. In 1833, he lost the remainder of his inheritance in a series of bank failures and for the first time had to start to work for his living, as a journalist. In 1836 he married Isabella Shawe: they had three children one of whom died in infancy. Isabella was mentally unstable and by 1840 Thackeray was forced to put her in a home. During the 1840s Thackeray's reputation as a writer grew, particularly for his contributions to the satirical periodical *Punch*. His most famous novel *Vanity Fair* appeared in monthly parts from 1847-8. He made two lecture tours to the USA, and founded the *Cornhill Magazine* in 1859. He also wrote a series of 'Christmas books', which he illustrated himself.

Trollope, Anthony (1815-82) novelist. His father failed in business and the family lived in poverty which made the young Trollope miserable at school at Harrow and Winchester. The family's fortunes improved after the death of his father, when his mother, Frances, embarked on a successful literary career. Trollope took a job in the Post Office, and in 1841 was sent to Ireland where he prospered. He married Rose Heseltine in 1844; they had two sons. Recognition as an author came with the publication of *The Warden* (1855), the first of the 'Barsetshire novels'. Trollope's other great sequence of novels was the 'Palliser novels' (1864-80). He retired from the Post Office in 1867: amongst his achievements was the introduction of the pillar box.

Wilde, Oscar (1854-1900) playwright. Born into a Protestant middle-class family in Ireland. His student career at Trinity College, Dublin and then at Oxford was extraordinary, winning major prizes both for Classics and for English verse. He was influenced by Walter Pater and J.M. Whistler and his connection with the Aesthetic Movement was soon established. He led a very public life, attracting the satirical attention, for example, of W.S. Gilbert (see page 78). He travelled and married; by 1886 there were two sons, Cyril and Vyvyan, and a house in Chelsea which was decorated at great length and expense. He was also, however, leaning more and more to homosexuality, and became involved in particular with a young poet, Lord Alfred Douglas. In 1895, at the height of his fame as a writer of society comedies, he was sent to prison for homosexual acts which were then illegal. On his release in 1897 he went into exile in France, where he died in Paris in 1900.

FURTHER READING

Chapter 1 The Victorian Age
Geoffrey Best *Mid-Victorian Britain 1851-75* (London 1971). Concentrates on social history.
Christopher Harvie and H.C.G. Matthew *Nineteenth Century Britain: A Very Short Introduction* (Oxford 2000). A good brief survey.
Eric Hobsbawm *Age of Revolution, Age of Capital* and *Age of Empire* (London 1962, 1975 and 1987). One of the best introductions to European history and culture in the 19th century.
Eric Hobsbawm and Terence Ranger (eds) *The Invention of Tradition* (Cambridge 1983). Particularly interesting for its essays on the monarchy by David Cannadine and Hobsbawm's own general essay on 'Mass-Producing Traditions: Europe, 1870-1914'.
K. Theodore Hoppen *New Oxford History of Britain*: *The Mid-Victorian Generation 1846-1886* (Oxford 1998)
Walter Houghton *The Victorian Frame of Mind* (New Haven 1957). A useful introduction to the thought of the period.
Anthony Wood *Nineteenth Century Britain 1815-1914* (2nd edition, London 1982)

Chapter 2 The Urban Scene
Peter Ackroyd *Dickens* (London 1990)
Asa Briggs *Victorian People* (London 1965), *Victorian Cities* (London 1968) and *Victorian Things* (London 1990). With information about the social background to Victorian literature.
Kathryn Hughes *George Eliot The Last Victorian* (London 1998)
P.J. Keating *Working Classes in Victorian Fiction* (London 1971)
Jeannette King *Tragedy in the Victorian Novel* (Cambridge 1979)
Donald Read *The Age of Urban Democracy 1868-1914* (London 1994)
Jenny Uglow *Elizabeth Gaskell: A Habit of Stories* (London 1993)

Chapter 3 Country Life
Michael Millgate *Thomas Hardy: A Biography* (London 1982)
Merryn Williams *Thomas Hardy and Rural England* (1972)

Chapter 4 Education and the Arts
Juliet Barker *The Brontës* (London 1994)
Roger Dixon and Stefan Muthesius *Victorian Architecture* (2nd edition, London 1985). A good basic introduction to the subject.
Andrew Graham-Dixon *History of British Art* (London 1996). Based on a BBC programme, it has a very thought-provoking chapter on the art of the period.

Ann Thwaite *Emily Tennyson: The Poet's Wife* (London 1996). Gives an alternative viewpoint on one of the writers covered in this book.
There are many books about Pre-Raphaelite art, and major collections in museums in London, Liverpool, Manchester, and Birmingham. It is also worth looking for Victorian buildings in your own area; there are major buildings in most large towns and cities. To find out about them try looking in *The Buildings of England* (Penguin), edited by Nikolaus Pevsner and others.

Chapter 5 Religion and Science
Gillian Beer *Darwin's Plots* (London 1983)
Victoria Glendinning *Trollope* (London 1992)
Robert Lee Wolff *Gains and Losses: Novels of Faith and Doubt in Victorian England* (London 1977)

Chapter 6 Victorian Drama
Richard Ellman *Oscar Wilde* (London 1987)
George Rowell *Victorian Drama 1792-1914* (2nd edition Cambridge 1978)
J.L. Styan *The English Stage* (Cambridge 1996)

General
Introductions to editions of novels and poems produced by Oxford University Press, Penguin Books and Everyman Classics are useful sources of information. The *Preface Books* (Longman) is a series of introductions to single authors which contain both biographical and literary information. The *Casebook* series (Macmillan) contains collections of critical essays. There are two series: the older one contains classic essays and some contemporary criticism, while the new series introduces more modern critical approaches. Two anthologies of contemporary writings and documents relating to the social and cultural history of the period were produced for Open University courses. *Nature and Industrialization* (Alasdair Clayre (ed.) 1977) covers the period from 1760-1860, while the latter part of Victoria's reign is mostly covered by *Culture and Society in Britain 1850-1890* (J.M. Golby (ed.) 1986). Useful information can also be found in *The Cambridge Companion to Victorian Poetry* edited by Joseph Bristow (2000) and *The Cambridge Companion to the Victorian Novel* edited by Deirdre David (2001).

Websites
The following websites are excellent gateways for further research in Victorian literature:

http://andromeda.rutgers.edu/~jlynch/Lit/victoria.html
http://65.107.211.206/vn/litov.html

INDEX